AF865431

SOTHIS PRESS

Sothis Press aims to completely reimagine the public domain book with an emphasis on universal access to captivatingly designed print editions. We believe that technology will enable every single book ever published to be perpetually accessible in beautiful print form. Sothis is beauty in ubiquity.

www.sothis.press
1 Waterhouse Square, London, EC1N 2ST

How to Save Money

The Care of Money, Plain Facts About Every Kind of Investment, an Expos? of the Prevalent Fraudulent and Get-Rich-Quick Schemes, Valuable and Authentic Information for All Moderate Money-Savers and Small Investors

Nathaniel C. Fowler, Jr.

SOTHIS PRESS

ISBN 978-1-0365-3217-8

This edition is published by
Sothis Press © 2023. The company
is registered in England and Wales.
The Company Number is 14900389.

How to Save Money

The Care of Money — Plain Facts About Every Kind of Investment — An Exposé of the Prevalent Fraudulent and Get-Rich-Quick Schemes — Valuable and Authentic Information for all Moderate Money-Savers and Small Investors

By

Nathaniel C. Fowler, Jr.

AUTHOR OF "STARTING IN LIFE," "PRACTICAL SALES-MANSHIP," ETC.

CHICAGO
A. C. McClurg & Co.
1912

Published February, 1912

W. F. Hall Printing Company
Chicago

PREFACE

THE writer of this book feels that it is advisable, although it may not be necessary, to announce positively that he is not connected, either directly or indirectly, with any form of investment, or with any bank or brokerage establishment, or with any institution having anything to do with the sale of stocks, bonds, or securities of any kind. He has no axe to grind at the reader's expense, no scheme to further, and no investment to recommend.

He is telling the truth, the whole truth, within the field of his light. He attempts to get at rock-bottom and to reach the sub-cellar of financial fact. He is aware that on all questions, and especially those of investment, opinions differ, and that most honest men cross swords when they attempt to appraise, value, and recommend.

What one reliable man considers a good form of investment, may not appeal to the judgment of another equally honest and cautious. He who has been successful in investing along a certain line will naturally favor that form of investment, while another, who thinks that he has been bitten, condemns a good thing, even though his injury may not have been caused by the unreliability of the investment itself.

No one is completely fair, and every one is somewhat biassed. Personal experience, natural or acquired conceit, pig-headedness or stubbornness, count mightily in framing opinion and in forming judgment.

All kinds of investments have some intrinsic value, save those which are highly fraudulent, but some give the maximum of security, while others have the minimum of it. Some are sound and solid, while others are purely speculative.

The saver and investor should bear always in mind this great fundamental point,— that the maximum of interest is usually accompanied with the minimum of security, and that the minimum of interest is likely to be close to the maximum of safety.

Good security seldom gives large profits.

The writer has strenuously avoided the exercise of mere personal opinion, and has made every effort to keep far away from individual bias. He has used every known precaution, and he hopes that he has succeeded.

To the little he knows, he has added the much of what he knows about what others know, and what he has written does not in any case represent his own unsupported opinion. He has dealt in majorities, and has been a strict adherent to the great law of averages, that everything that he has said may have the strength of the composite.

The book is not intended for large investors, or for professional money-changers, or for speculators. It is addressed, primarily, to men and women of every age who are financially able to save moderately and systematically, and who wish to learn, therefore, of every form of investment, that they may place their money with the maximum of safety.

CONTENTS

Contents

How to Save Money

How To Save Money

CHAPTER I

THE MATERIALISTIC

THE critical readers of this book,— and I hope there will be many of them,— may honestly feel that I have leaned altogether too heavily toward the purely materialistic at a sacrifice of the mental and spiritual and that which counts more in the up-lifting and betterment of humanity.

Money, together with those things for which money stands, is largely located within the physical or materialistic field; for money, by itself, is certainly of neither ethical, mental, nor spiritual composition, and is, as much as anything else, representative of the material.

I do not apologize, however, for the policy of this book. The material plays by no means a secondary part on the stage of everyday life. If God found it necessary in creating the mental and spiritual man to build material headquarters for the housing of the mind and the soul, we have no right to ignore either of the departments of Divine construction.

It is unnecessary to make a comparison between

the higher things and the lower things in which the higher things are kept. One without the other would not present, in this world, a completed whole. Therefore, as both are found together, one may be considered as essential to human life as the other.

This world, preëminently material in its construction, should be considered and appreciated. It is, for the time being, the physical dwelling-place of the spiritual man. The Almighty placed us here for a purpose, and would not have given us physical land, and food, and other things as material, if they were not to be used by us and made to serve their ordained purposes.

There will be neither money nor business in millennial days, for all things worth having will then be used, not abused. But for the present, and probably for many generations to come, money will play a prominent part, and the making and saving of money will be necessary for present existence and future protection.

To ignore money and money-saving, because they may be purely materialistic, so long as they are necessary to human existence, is foolish and criminally wrong.

It is impossible properly to develop and maintain the better part of man without careful housing. Food, a roof, and fire will be essential so long as we must eat and keep dry and warm. And these things, which some think are man's natural heritage, at the present time are procurable only by the expenditure of money.

Despise money if you will, and certainly it deserves to be despised, for, in itself, it is the cause of nearly every crime; but do not forsake money which is obtained honestly and may be profitably used. Unless we return to Nature, as, perhaps, Nature intended, we will have to get money or starve to death.

A vessel, freighted with the necessities of life and many of those things which appeal to our higher nature, was stranded on an unknown island. A storm had made her unseaworthy, but her hull held together long enough for her cargo to be brought ashore. Everything was saved, including cases of beautiful paintings and other works of art, and books that live and talk. The captain was a man of education, but he never could have handled his vessel, if he had not kept his feet on deck while he looked into the clouds. The disaster was no fault of his. Did he order the works of art to be first landed? Certainly not. They came last, and before them, lumber, and stoves, and food. Under his direction houses were built, with roofs that did not leak. Stoves were set up, beds made, and the strongest building of all contained the food supplies. A well was dug, everything necessary for the physical body was arranged for. Then, and not until then, the works of art were taken and placed upon the walls, to add a touch of beauty to the bareness of the material. The house, with a roof that did not leak, came first. The physical man was attended to before any effort was made to please the eye or æsthetic taste. The better things were ignored until there was a material place to keep them in.

I told this story in a lecture once, and a man with a long coat, a high collar, and a white necktie arose from the audience. He took highly respectable exceptions to what I had said, for this kind of man is never strenuous in thought or action. He claimed that he would rather have the landscape than the land. He enlarged upon the ethical and reduced the material. When he had finished, I remarked that the man who loved the landscape more than the land found it necessary to stand on somebody else's land that he might see everybody's landscape, and this sort of a man is dishonest, because he is willing to view the free and beautiful things of life at the expense of the hard-working man who bought the land for the visionist to stand upon.

I wanted to use the language of the street, and say that this landscape man was a "dead-beat," who was willing to "beat" his way to a free landscape.

So long as we live largely by the expenditure of money, either we earn that money ourselves, or we are paupers. Many a man, who keeps his eyes turned continuously toward the sky, has no respect for the workers who are laboring to keep him on earth. It is dishonest not to support ourselves and provide for the future, unless we are physically and mentally unable to do so.

I am not asking any man to accumulate large sums of money, for few high-grade men ever do. But I am attempting to show that money-earning and money-saving are positively essential under present conditions, and that the refusal to earn money or to save money, when it can be done, is criminally dishonest, as dishonest as it is to steal your neighbor's house or your neighbor's bank.

If you are able to earn your living, and are able to save money, and do not, you are a voluntary pauper, unworthy of the respect of man.

When you refuse to do these things, you simply and deliberately say to the world that you are willing to live by the sweat of others' brows and by the work of others' hands.

Look into the sky, if you will, love and reverence art, think more of the purity of real beauty than you do of the purely material, but first build a house with a roof that does not leak. If you do not, the rain will wash over your canvases, and the sun will warp your higher thoughts.

The material cannot be built upon the spiritual, but the spiritual lives and thrives upon the material.

Never forget the need of a house with a roof that does not leak.

CHAPTER *II*

THE PROVIDENT AND IMPROVIDENT

BOTH the spendthrift and the miser are plain, simple, and ordinary fools of the most conventional sort. There is not even the flicker of a spark of originality, progress, or of anything else which stands for anything worth while, in their everyday folly. They do not deserve, and they never receive, the respect of anybody, not even of their own kind.

The spendthrift, in the whirl of the world, never meets a friend; and the miser, in his seclusion, is too unsocial even to see the reflection of himself.

The spendthrift over-pays for everything which he receives. It is impossible for him to obtain equitable return for the money he distributes. He sows, but never harvests. He works harder in the field of his folly than do the toilers of the soil.

The miser is a storehouse with a hundred entrances and without an exit. He is a receiver, not a contributor. He and the spendthrift are menaces to society, and a court of sensible equity and common justice, if it could be established, would sentence both of them to hard and active labor — to doing something which would be a contribution to general humanity.

It has been said (but, of course, the statement cannot be substantiated by statistical fact) that more than half of the great middle class of people, especially Americans, are improvident, that they spend all that they earn, that half of them attempt to put out more than they take in, and that they live close to their incomes, or ahead of them, flush to-day and cramped to-morrow.

Whether or not the proportion given is as large, I will not attempt to say, but that it is of considerable dimension would appear to be self-evident.

Practically every physician will admit that he loses from twenty-five to forty per cent of his bills, especially from the middle class of people, and that the lower grade of patients are likely to be of more financial profit to him than are those who fly regularly for shelter under the protecting wing of conventional respectability.

The retail grocer, and others who cater to family trade, and the credit-giving tailor, especially, are obliged to use the utmost caution if they would avoid continuous loss.

The establishment of commercial agencies, credit associations, and trade-protecting orders of every kind, furnish *prima facie* evidence that a heavy proportion of the people at large are both dishonest and improvident.

The reader may feel that I am pessimistic, and that I am looking upon the dark side of things. The pages of this book are intended to be printed mirrors of fact, reflecting actualities, true statements of conditions that are, not conditions as we would like to have them. I would suggest that the doubter interview the retail merchant, and others, including the house-renters and the sellers of those things which appeal to the alleged better class of society. He may then feel that I have leaned rather toward the optimistic than to the pessimistic view.

Why do people live beyond their means, especially those with incomes sufficient to provide all of the necessities and most of the comforts of life? There is not, and cannot be, any good reason. At best, there is but a feeble excuse,— the exemplification of that false, and yet common, idea possessed even by those who have some brains of fair quality, that, because the world is popularly supposed to judge by appearances, and to reckon us by the outward show we make of ourselves, and to honor the superficial side of life, we are justified in appearing to be what we are not at an expense which we have no right to allow ourselves to assume.

This false conception of things, coupled with the bad judgment accompanying it, is largely responsible for the present deplorable condition of society, although, of course, the real source lies in the lack of personal honor, a quality which is far from becoming universal.

As a matter of fact this reason, or excuse, for living up to our incomes, or beyond them, is without tangible or locatable foundation, for the spendthrift, or the extravagant man, is an all-around loser and a criminal before the bar of humanity; and, further, he receives no real recognition from those before whom he makes his display, no, not even from his kind.

The sinner, whether his wrong-doing be extravagance, or something not quite so bad, or worse, is a product of vulgarity and corruption, a back-biter, a gossiper, and a busy-body, who, from some normal or abnormal reason, has not what may be considered sense enough to observe in others the very sin he, himself, commits. Therefore, the spendthrift, or his extravagant associate, fails to obtain what he desires,— a position in society, a recognition of what he wants people to think he is. The only benefit that accrues to him, if it may be so called, is that he enjoys artificially some of the luxuries which his sensible neighbor is not willing to have unless he can afford them. He does not, as a spendthrift, or as a representative of extravagant living, obtain a single true friend, and he never receives any real admiration.

The friend who loves us because he is allowed to help us spend our money, or benefits by the expenditure of that money, or who admires us because we have money, does not represent, in fact, even the shadow of the semblance of the stuff friendship is made of. Friends cannot be purchased by money, and dealers in friendship refuse to be money-changers.

A show of extravagance never did anybody any good, and never will. True friendship occurs only in a reciprocating way, and depends wholly upon genuine character. The extravagant man receives absolutely nothing, except the ignoble satisfaction which the exercise of over-expenditure gives to one who will not, or does not, think.

The improvident man is usually a chronic borrower. He lives upon what he earns, and upon what he can get without earning it. He may or may not intend to make good. If he can, without an effort, he is likely to do so. If he cannot, he thinks little about it. The little he has left of his conscience is kept in cold storage and melts in the sunlight.

A large proportion of improvident people refuse to save when they have the opportunity.

They live beyond their means. They would not sacrifice any part of the present for the protection of the future, and yet they expect the provident to help them when disaster comes.

Let me illustrate by a concrete example: Two young men of equal ability, but not of equal character, start to travel the great highway of life. For a dozen years their incomes are the same, and there should be no material difference in their expenses. One allows himself to enjoy the luxuries of life, and at the end of the period he is dollarless. The other has been provident, but not mean. He has lived below his income, and has accumulated some money. The improvident man, who has lived better and enjoyed the luxuries of life, expects the provident man, who has made sacrifices, to share his savings with him. In other words, the spendthrift who has spent his money,— eaten it and drunk it,— asks the man who has saved to give part of his savings to him. He has eaten the whole of his pie, and demands a part of the other fellow's pie. This condition is too prevalent to be a novelty.

It is self-evident that we cannot have money and spend it at the same time. The ever-ready spender does not accumulate, while the systematic saver protects himself against the future.

There would appear to be no reason why the

provident man should share his hard-earned savings with the improvident man, who could and would have been in the same position in which the provident man is, if he had exercised the same care and made the same sacrifices.

The sinner cannot escape punishment, and withholding deserved penalties, unless there be sufficient counteracting repentance, is neither fair nor equitable.

The improvident man deserves to suffer. Let him suffer. He has earned a penalty. Let him have it. Better that he suffer ten times over than that the careful man make an undue sacrifice for the benefit of one who threw away what he had.

I know that I am making strong statements, and that some of my readers may misunderstand me, and, perhaps, I am giving them some opportunity to feel that I do not look upon charity as the greatest virtue of all virtues. Let me, right here, assure these readers that I think I have an appreciation of charity, and of what charity stands for. Without charity, and the love it represents, this world would be a desert without oasis, and across it would flow no stream of living water. Charity is the very warp and woof of all there is worth having. But charity, distributed promiscuously, and given as a reward for crime, is really an abetter of crime, and does harm where it intended to do good.

There are times when we should help the improvident man, on account of the innocent members of his family, who may be free from fault. To aid him as a part of the suffering family is often justifiable, but to help him, alone, when his present condition is due to his voluntary acts, is not charity at all, and is, at best, of no stronger stuff than the distilled essence of diluted and sentimental philanthropy.

The man who is financially embarrassed because of extravagance, and because he would not save when he could save, does not deserve financial assistance when the inevitable crash comes, and any attempt on the part of the provident man to relieve him financially, unless such relief benefits an innocent family, is not only foolish, but often criminally wrong.

Do not misunderstand me. I am not referring to the man who is suffering because of the inevitable,— from conditions which were beyond his control,— but to the spendthrift, the voluntarily improvident, he who has lived up to his income, or beyond it, when he had more than sufficient to take care of him, and who is now suffering from his own voluntary misdeeds. Such a man deserves no financial help until he has redeemed himself by the sweat of his brow and the strain of his muscle. He is not an object of charity or of philanthropy, and he who loves to help others had better turn the tide of his goodness into other channels, that he may aid the millions of those who are thrown overboard, and who did not sink voluntarily.

There are enough good men, temporarily or permanently in disaster, to furnish all the material philanthropists need for the exercise of their generosity.

To help the deserving is right. To aid the undeserving is wrong; yes, doubly wrong, because the undeserving deserves no help, and the helping of the undeserving robs the deserving of his due.

Giving more than opportunity to those who are too lazy to grasp it, is to encourage carelessness, extravagance, and sin.

Those who do their best are worthy of all praise and aid, but those who will not do their best should suffer the self-imposed penalty. You have no right to do for another what he did not do for himself, when he comes to you and wants you to do for him what he could have done for himself and would not do.

I have no pity for the man who won't. I have every sympathy for the man who will.

He who tries to do his best is a success, no matter what the result may be; but he who does not try to do his best has no right to expect the man who did his best to share with him the product of his labor, judgment, and sacrifice.

Help those who help themselves, or who try to help themselves, and refuse to aid those who with closed eyes have walked in the light, and who with open ears have refused to hear the warning thunders of danger.

CHAPTER III

LIVING BEYOND OUR MEANS

I DO not think that I am far away from the truth when I say that experience and observation make me believe that about seventy-five per cent of city dwellers and that about twenty per cent of the inhabitants of country towns spend all that they earn, and that at least one-half of them have lived or are living beyond their means.

Instead of conditions changing for the better, they appear to be going the other way. Probably more people are to-day living beyond their means than there were yesterday, and there seems to be little inclination on their part to practise any sort of economy. Not only do they spend all they earn, but they anticipate their incomes or salaries, incurring indebtedness in advance of possibility of payment.

It is obvious that a family of small income, and with legitimate necessary expenses, cannot always do much better than break even, though it practise the most stringent economy; but it is a fact that the majority of people spend all that they make, or live beyond their incomes.

The necessities of life, and most of those things

which are considered comforts, are not excessively expensive. Most of us can live comfortably on very much less money than is supposed to be necessary for right living. Foundation expenses are small, over-head excesses are large, and most of the latter contribute very little to anything worth while.

Getting behind is usually due to extravagance or to an unwillingness to do without the unnecessary.

True, no sharp line can be drawn between the cost of comfort and the cost of extravagance, for what may appear to be an extravagance for one person may be a seeming necessity for another. But one who cares, and who honestly desires to succeed, will not find it difficult to discriminate, and will invariably recognize the difference between the necessary and the unnecessary.

Fully one-half of the financial failures are due to pure and simple extravagance in the home and to expenditure of money for personal pleasures entirely removed from necessity. Many a man, who manages his business with anxious care, handles his personal expenses in the most extravagant and foolish way.

Not only are home and personal expenses the cause of half of the business failures, but they are in many cases the prime source of home troubles, leading to the breaking up of the home and covering nearly every form of family unpleasantness.

While money appears to be more a part of business than of home life, the foundation of economy, or of extravagance, or of sensible or senseless expenditure, is laid in the home. Here one first begins to save money or to do the reverse.

The economical-home man or woman is usually economical in business.

Home extravagance, particularly that of clothes, has its basis in a desire to make what the world foolishly calls a good appearance,—to decorate the outside without regard to the condition or the necessity. In fact, I think that to this almost insane desire to make a so-called good appearance is due most of our extravagance in dress, in furnishings, in decorations, and in the purchase of things more for show than for utility and comfort. Indeed, the display of extravagance is always superficial. We wish to appear well before our friends and neighbors, who we think would judge us superficially. As a matter of fact any undue attempt on our part to dress or live beyond our means works in a direction opposite to our intentions. We are not judged as superficially as we think we are. Most of us, particularly if we are of the middle class, are pretty fairly well sized-up by our friends and acquaintances. They either know what our income is, or can come pretty close to it. If we over-dress ourselves, they despise us, even though they may be as guilty as we are.

If we cannot afford to keep horses or automobiles, and we do so, we lose the respect of horse-keepers and automobilists, even though they may have less right than we have to drive horses or run motor-cars.

The shoddy man has no respect for his kind. If he is shoddy, he recognizes the quality in all those who are shoddy.

It is impossible to understand that peculiar trait in human nature, which encourages one to "show off," so to speak, among those who know that one is "showing off." It would seem that nothing is to be gained by pretending to be what we are not to those who know that we are not what we pretend to be. For example, let us suppose that Mr. John Smith is Mr. John Jones's employer, and that Mrs. Smith invites Mrs. Jones to tea. Mrs. Smith knows the size of the Jones income; therefore, she is in a position to judge whether or not her guest is dressed properly and within her means. It is quite probable that the wife of the employee will wear better and more expensive clothes than those worn by the employer's wife. Instead of Mrs. Smith being impressed by Mrs. Jones's clothing, she despises the woman for living beyond the family income, and carries her disgust to her husband, to the detriment of Mr. John Jones.

May I forget honesty for a moment that I may more closely analyze pretence, which is the top, bottom, sides, and centre of the cause for living beyond our means? Let me consider pretence, for the time being, as a commodity with intrinsic value. If it be a commodity, and if it have intrinsic value, then it is valuable only in so far as it is not recognized as pretence, but is considered as representative of fact.

If one cares nothing for truth and honesty, then he may use pretence to some advantage, provided always that he can mask it effectively, and can force it to appear what it is not. This, however, is impossible for any one to accomplish.

The pretender is always the loser, in the long run surely, in the short run usually. The cold-blooded world will weigh him correctly, sooner or later.

There is absolutely nothing to be gained by living beyond one's means: First, because it prevents one from protecting oneself in case of emergency; Secondly, because it is a precarious habit and sets a bad example; Thirdly, because it necessitates economy in some directions, which may be dangerous to health and comfort; Fourthly, because, instead of giving the credit and producing the impression desired, it always results in the opposite; Fifthly, because it is the forerunner of almost certain failure; Sixthly, it is positively dishonest; Seventhly, because its action always injures and never accomplishes anything.

We are what we are, and we are taken usually for what we are, except for a transient period or by people whose respect is worth less than nothing. We have what others think we have, and any attempt on our part to produce the impression of possessing more than we really have, can give only a boomerang result.

Living beyond one's means is not only wrong, but extremely foolish. Even the most extravagant and foolish have not a particle of respect for their own kind, and in their hearts they admire those who have sense enough to live within their incomes.

One of the best places for the study of human nature, and for the weighing of values, is at the summer resort, especially at the summer hotel, not necessarily of the better grade, but of the highest price. Fully seven-eighths of the over-dressed men and women, and of those who come in automobiles, represent neither wealth nor social position. The probabilities are that the plainer dressed people, even though they comprise but a small per cent of the guests, collectively have a dozen times more money and more than a dozen times higher social standing.

I am aware, of course, that practically all of the multi-millionaires, and all of their families, are devotees to show and style and to the display of every form of foolish and financially criminal extravagance.

The tendency for show on the part of our wealthiest people is growing rapidly, because display offers opportunity for competition, and few men would care for very large sums of money if great wealth did not give them the chance to vulgarly parade it.

But we need not draw our lesson from these over-monied people. Although they seem to be numerous, they are in an almost microscopic minority.

Most of us compete only with our class or with one just above us. Competition means expenditure, either of energy or money, or of both. Competition has its right place in every department of human affairs; for, when considered properly, it may be an incentive, a pusher and puller, leading to better things; but when its action is devoted wholly to show purposes, and I am using the word "show" advisedly, it is a menace to good society, disgusting and dangerous, and productive of the worst result.

Those who live beyond their means, and by that I do not mean getting in debt where there is no help for it, are positively dishonest as well as supremely foolish. Nothing is to be gained. It means the stifling of conscience, the loss of respect, the annihilation of economy, the production and development of extravagance, and stands for the ruin of the home, and the breaking down of the business. It accomplishes absolutely nothing in the round-up. Its maintenance neither creates nor holds the impression desired. It gives no return for the expenditure.

May I not paraphrase the old rule? It might truly read,

"By their extravagance may we know that they are not what they seem to be!"

CHAPTER IV

FIXED EXPENSES

EVERYBODY, except the pauper, receives his material necessities, comforts, and luxuries by the expenditure of money. This money is expended either systematically or promiscuously. If the former it is known as a fixed expense, settled upon with premeditation and with an appreciation of financial responsibility.

The successful man invariably lives and works under a fixed expense, allowing himself to expend for a year, or for any other period, approximately what he has laid aside or proportioned for the purpose. For example, he decides that be can afford to live at a cost of four thousand dollars a year, and he does not allow himself to exceed that amount for regular living expenses. If he has much money saved up, or an unexpected thousand dollars comes in, he may decide to purchase an automobile or to take a trip to Europe; but he does not consider either as a part of his fixed expenses. They are extras, and are allowed to occur only as extras and not as a part of the regular cost of living. In this way he knows where he stands, regulates his outgo to his income, exceeding it only when conditions either demand or suggest an extra expenditure.

This fixed-expense principle is carried into his business and into all his financial transactions. If he be extravagant, his extravagance is not allowed to be a part of what he considers the regular cost of living.

It is the duty of every one, whether his income be ten dollars a week or ten thousand a month, to establish a fixed expense, a definite scale of expenditure, and to keep within that no matter how much he may spend as extras, considering every dollar beyond the amount appropriated as not a part of living or necessary expense, but as a justifiable, foolish, or criminal extravagance. Even the latter, bad as it is, is not so disastrous if it is prepared for and the responsibility of it realized. Financial failure is usually due, not to thought-out and premeditated action, but to thoughtlessness and carelessness in expenditure, to hit-or-miss speculation, and to that prevalent and chronic disease known as taking chances.

Men who think and care may do wrong, but men who do not care, never do right, especially in financial matters.

CHAPTER V

HOW MUCH TO SAVE

NOW much should a young man, a single man, a to-be-married man, a married man, a man of any age, or a corresponding girl or woman, put aside as a saving or investment fund each week, each month, or each year, or during any other selected period?

To establish either a set or general rule for anybody, save oneself, would be unreasonable and unfair, and, really, I doubt if it could be done at all.

It is obvious that the multi-millionaire, with an annual income of millions of dollars, more or less, can save ninety-nine per cent of his profits, and yet keep the wolf of poverty from getting any nearer to him than an adjoining street. It is self-evident that the family man, whose wages are but a few hundred dollars a year, cannot put aside more than a small percentage of his earnings, or not more than a microscopic part of them, if he would give himself and his family the common and ordinary necessities of life, luxuries never to cross his threshold.

No percentage rule, or any other rule, can be

established with this inequality of income, and with the extreme variation of living expenses, and while men who deserve to succeed, succeed and fail, and undeserving men meet with the same fate.

When we live as we should live (and that means close to Nature), when we become satisfied with legitimate comforts, and rightly abhor extremes in luxury and inexcusable extravagances, we may then establish a somewhat universal footing, and a standard of living, which will admit of the framing and keeping of some definite rule of saving.

The condition of our present status of semi-civilization makes it easy for one man to put aside a large proportion of what he earns or otherwise receives, and utterly impossible for another, who works as hard or harder, and who is in every way as deserving or more so, to approach anywhere near him, proportionately, in the amount of his savings.

Therefore, it would appear to be impossible to establish a law of saving, or to form any general rule of giving, and this condition will remain until the people at large become more advanced, and are mentally able to grasp and properly weigh true values, and become intelligent enough to give as much credit to the man who does what he can, be it ever so little, as to the one who accumulates a dozen times more money, because it is more than a dozen times easier for him to do so.

Many a dollar-saver makes a greater effort to assemble and hold his single dollar, than does the hundred-dollar man, who finds saving as easy as spending.

A more terrible commentary could not be made upon the mischievous quality and contemptible charity of our modern brand of adulterated justice, than the placing of the name of the heaviest giver in quantity at the head of the subscription paper, and thereby measuring the generosity of man, even in the Church itself, by the amount he gives of his property, and not by what he gives of himself.

The one rule of saving that can be established is,— that it is the duty of every one who can save, to save all he can, provided he does not sacrifice a greater duty by so doing.

Perhaps I can make it a little plainer. It is one's duty to save all he can *economically* save, for there is such a thing as extravagance in saving. To save more than one should save is meanness; to save less than one should save is criminal. True economy stands for the good of all concerned, and demands an appropriate saving, neither more nor less. It forbids parsimony, and is equally opposed to any sort of extravagance, or to any accumulation of abnormal proportions.

Few of us, unless we have experienced poverty, or have lived close to it, have any adequate understanding or realization of the purchasing and sustaining power of the moderate income, or of a small sum of money, which will do, if permitted, much more than it is usually allowed to aecomplish, and is sufficient for systematic and continuous saving.

I do not apologize for venturing the assertion that the great middle class of people wastes a third of what it spends, taking people as they run; that is to say, that most folks would receive substantially the same amount of necessities, comforts, and pleasures, if they paid out two-thirds of the money they now spend or otherwise distribute, and saved the balance.

No matter how extravagantly inclined we may be; no matter how much we may love money, and the good and bad things money will give us, we cannot occupy more than one bed at a time, nor wear more than one suit of clothes at once, nor does good society demand that we carry many spare beds or own more than a few suits of clothes. The necessities of life consist of the fulfilment of but a few conditions:

First, Something to eat.

Secondly, A place to live in.

Thirdly, Proper clothes.

Fourthly, Proper care when sick or disabled.

Beyond these things, the physical body demands nothing, however much it may want something. The present and economic conditions, however, add a Fifthly, that of some provision for emergencies and the future; and the better part of us, — our minds,— requires a Sixthly, that of mental food, and opportunity to receive those things which stand for something beyond the physical, and which reach out to the betterment of mankind, — education, development, and enlightenment.

Something to eat costs comparatively little, if we would confine ourselves to wholesome food, the kind of food worth eating. The costly table is maintained at the sacrifice not only of digestion and health, but money as well.

A place to live in need not heavily tax one's income, except in cities where there seem to be compulsory extravagances, and many of the so-called compulsory extravagances can be avoided.

Appropriate and comfortable clothes are essential, but well-dressing does not demand half the expense that most people think it does. It is remarkable how the application of care and sense will reduce the size of the clothing bills. It has been said that the rich spend less for clothes than does the average member of the middle class, who seems to be laboring under that popular and prevalent delusion that appearances, and extravagance with its accompanying cost, are necessary to social standing. I am inclined to take exceptions to this view, because the average millionaire and his family are likely to be foolishly extravagant, and to care as much for vulgar show as does the society man of little money, who would appear wealthy. This devotion to appearances, often carried over the line of sanity, is responsible for ninety per cent of the inexcusable waste and tinsel show of the world. But the man of money, who does not need to be a spendthrift, is often more addicted to show than are those who have the flimsy excuse for doing it,— that they may be reckoned to be more than they are.

Over-dressing, and any other form of extravagance, injures rather than helps one's reputation, for the over-dressed and showy man and woman are plain and simple fools, and sometimes I think they deserve pity more than condemnation. With extravagance all about them and on them, they criticise freely, and invariably condemn their neighbors for doing what they do themselves.

Any attempt at over-dressing is not only wrong

in principle, but it is pure idiocy. It gives no prestige, no real satisfaction, either to the party himself or to those who see him. Its benefits, if there are any, are of purely imaginary growth.

Extravagance in dress is more to be condemned than over-expenditure in any other direction, for it does no good to anybody in any way. There is no excuse for it. It is primarily responsible for improvidence. It places a mortgage on the future. It incurs an indebtedness which is seldom paid, for equity and right are sure to foreclose, and at a time when the debtor is least able to stand the strain.

Saving is necessary, that the sick and disabled may be cared for. Sickness comes in the night, and accident is likely to occur at any time. The future is always with us, as well as beyond us. It bears a significance for the present equalled only by the present itself.

The future is in the hands of the present, and is not likely to prosper unless the present provides for it.

We must either meet the future or die, and we cannot meet it properly or economically unless we foresee its demands and prepare for it.

In no other way can we provide for the future than by saving in the present, by putting aside things which the future will require. To fail to do this, if we can do it, is to commit a sin against ourselves and against our neighbor.

There is likely to be little over-expenditure along mental lines. True, the bookworm, who only crawls through life, is as big a fool as the man who lives in the fields of gold. Occasionally some one pays for education more than it is worth; for the mind-filling craze, which breaks one's health, which over-works the brain, even if the doer did what he did from good motives, is one of the worst forms of extravagance. It is no better than the placing of good things in a storehouse incapable of taking care of them.

This fighting one's way through college, to obtain an education at the cost of health, is to be deplored. One had better be strong and healthy, with a body vigorous enough to use an untrained mind, than attempt to work a brain-full of education, with a frame too weak to carry it.

The good of all training is in its distribution, — in the use that is made of it,— and the receiver of a college education, who is unable to distribute it, has wasted his time and money, and others' time, in the getting of his education.

The first and best thing for a man to do is to locate his level, and ascertain what he can do and what he cannot do, to find out what he needs and what he does not need, and then to adjust his rate of expenditure to it. It may or may not absorb his income, and it may or may not allow him to save.

Any attempt to live beyond our means adds nothing to our reputation and takes much away from it, for the world, filled as it is with the superficial, is sure, sooner or later, to reckon us for what we are and to level us unmercifully to our proper plane before it gets through with us, or before we get through with it.

It is our duty, first, to take care of ourselves to-day; and, secondly, to prepare for to-morrow. To carry out the second proposition does not mean a sacrifice of to-day's necessities, for the responsibilities of to-day must be met whether or not there be something left over for to-morrow. But when one has more than enough for present necessities, he is a criminal before every bar of justice, if he does not provide for to-morrow.

Take care of to-day first, then take care of to-morrow, but do not forget that your prime duty is to provide for to-morrow after you have properly taken care of to-day.

Not to save when one can save is a refusal to make a reasonable sacrifice for the sake of the future. It places a man in the criminal class and suggests the advisability of framing a law which will prescribe a punishment beyond the natural penalty always accompanying improvidence.

He who will not save when he can save, and save all that he should save, not only robs himself and his family, if he has one, but deliberately, voluntarily, and intentionally becomes a menace to society, a member of the chain gang of paupers, of those who must rely upon others or perish when disaster arrives.

Considerably more than half of the married couples begin married life with a capital limited to the clothes they wear and sometimes they are deeply in debt; and yet they allow themselves to enter the most holy state given to man or woman without any preparation for the future, which they voluntarily leave entirely unprotected.

Of course none of these improvident people are in love with their mates, for true love is cautious and reasonably intelligent, and refuses to take unnatural chances, and never fails to provide for a probable future. They mistake infatuation for love, and without thinking about it, they foster the idea that two may live for the price of one. Nothing can be more illogical, nor more carelessly founded upon the quicksands of folly.

If I were permitted to make a few laws, I would formulate one prohibiting marriage until one or both of the contracting parties had saved sufficient money to pay reasonable expenses for a year. I know that I am shocking the sentimentalists, particularly those who love to be shocked, and who prattle and talk about the love they have never felt and do not understand.

The man who is not willing to save before marriage enough to maintain himself and his wife for a year has not sufficient energy and character to suggest that he is worthy to become a husband and father; nor is he in love with his wife, for love always protects, and love is never blind. Sentiment may be without eyes or near-sighted, but love does not have to wear spectacles.

The man who will not make a sacrifice in order to properly protect a probable family mistakes passion and selfishness for love, or else he is a fool; and the fool has no right to marry.

It is easier to save money before one is married than it is to do so afterwards, because living expenses are less, or should be so. The man who will not save without the coöperation of his economical wife, and must be coerced into doing right, is an unsafe proposition, and ought to be relegated to an enforced bachelorhood.

Premature marriages, occurring before proper provision is made for the future, are the cause of millions of break-downs and down-falls, and are primarily responsible for family wrecks, and often for divorces and every kind of dissipation.

It is the duty of every one to establish an economical policy, which will compel him to save the difference between his income and what is actually essential for living. For example, if a couple can live with a reasonable degree of comfort on a thousand dollars a year, and their income is fifteen hundred dollars, then it is their duty to save five hundred dollars, and to continue this proportionate saving until they have accumulated a fund which appears to be large enough to meet any condition likely to arise, including business failure and old age. To save up to this point is right and necessary. To accumulate beyond it shows avariciousness, a low character, a contemptible and inexcusable lack of public spirit, and no respect for the common decencies of life.

I am speaking harshly, because I feel that I am right, and I do not apologize to anybody. If I am wrong, then lay the blame at the door of my sincerity and to the long reviewing of experiences with thousands of people.

Over-saving is as bad as under-saving, perhaps even worse, because there may be an apparent excuse, although I doubt it, for not saving when one can save, while there is absolutely not even the faintest shadow of reason for over-accumulation.

Under-saving robs the man and his family, and creates expense for the town. Over-saving debauches the community.

No one has a right to save beyond a sum which will give ample provision for his future, unless he is accumulating for a specific and laudable purpose. It is his duty to continue to save until he has reached the point of protection.

Many of us can save much more than we think that we can, not by eliminating the necessities of life, but by cutting corners, so to speak.

If one has a desire to save, he will find many more opportunities to do so than he had at first thought existed.

What we want to do, we generally do; many of our wants, however, are purely imaginary.

A desire to save, and an appreciation of the value of protection, will invariably find a way of accomplishment, unless conditions absolutely forbid.

It is better to save a penny a day for the sake of principle, than not to save at all. There are few of us who cannot put away a cent a day, and if a cent is all that can be saved, save it systematically.

If you would command the respect of your employer, the respect of your neighbor, and the respect of the world at large, save, and save persistently, and be known as a provident man. Not only will you receive self-satisfaction and protection, but you will be better liked and be more respected by everybody, even by the superficial.

The bad man is not respected or loved by those of his kind, and the extravagant man, the man who can and will not save, is not only a knave, but a consummate fool, and he is so considered by those above him, with him, and beneath him.

The saver, who systematically puts aside even the smallest sum, creates by so doing a definite asset, which has a value beyond its intrinsic worth, for it helps to establish reputation and is the badge of character, integrity, and good sense.

The very principle of saving, itself, irrespective of the amount saved, if one saves all he can, puts the saver into a higher class, and gives him a tangible something which helps him to live better in the present and which protects him in the future.

Men who save are men of mark; men who do not save are marked men.

CHAPTER VI

EXTRAVAGANCE

THERE is not even a shadow of a semblance of excuse, right, and reason for any form or kind of extravagance. It works injury to everything it comes in contact with, has never accomplished anything for the good of anybody, nor has it contributed the gentlest push to the slowest propulsion of the slightest progress.

Extravagance does not possess a single redeeming quality. It is bad in substance and in principle. It has no place in human affairs, except to injure and to demoralize. It gives no return to anybody save transient pleasure, or, rather, the imitation of it, which, like the over-drinking of wine, is more than counteracted by disastrous results.

Meanness is not a part of extravagance. It has nothing in common with it. It is a sin in itself, and inexcusable; yet, bad as it is, it possesses but a small percentage of the evil contained in extravagance.

The injury meanness does may be confined to itself, and to those who come in immediate contact with it, while extravagance is a public sin confined to no narrow boundary and making always for general harm.

Economy is as far removed from meanness, from extravagance, and from those things which both stand for, as sunshine is opposed to midnight darkness.

Economy is one of the necessities and essentials of life. Without it permanent progress is impossible, and no work worth while can be accomplished.

Economy is the world's preservative. Without it everything is spoiled.

Economy and saving are closely allied, because without the former the latter could not exist.

Saving is the result of economy, although the principle of economy underlies saving.

The practice of true economy results in proper accumulation,— not too large and not too little, for economy has no sympathy with the miser and no mercy for the spendthrift.

The difference between success and failure may be found in the analysis of economy and extravagance.

Progress itself is founded upon economy, even upon strict economy, because of the power it has over the character of the people.

Hoarding is not economy. The miser is but a storehouse. He receives, but does not distribute.

Economy in business, and in everything else, accumulates that it may direct and meet the exigencies of famine. It does not obtain for the sake of keeping; it saves in the present that it may properly protect the future.

The practice of economy is due to an appreciation of the necessity of self-preservation combined with the desire to progress properly and to build a suitable foundation.

Nobody ever amounted to anything, either in business or out of business, in the professions, or in any other walk in life, from the framing of law to the making of shoes, unless he was a successful economist, as able to save as to spend. I am not referring wholly to financial saving, but to economy in the broadest sense; for one can be a sort of economist, and successful in a way, if he is not able to make or to save money. Many a professionalist lacks the ability to accumulate money. Money to him seems to be an unknown quantity, hard to get and easy to get rid of. He does not, or will not, save money; he may, however, be a success, because, while he is deficient in financial acumen, he may be proficient in economy. He may systematically and persistently store himself full of some material,— some kind of useful knowledge,— and in this direction he may practise and maintain a true economy with an absence of extravagance so far as conserving and distributing this mental commodity are concerned. If he did not do this, that is, practise economy along his line of action, he would amount to nothing.

It is a fact that financial success or business accomplishment is utterly impossible without basic, systematic, and persistent saving, the continuous practice of financial economy, without more than an occasional appearance of extravagance, until one has amassed a fortune.

Extravagance in money matters, and in all else, particularly if continuous, invites failure, and the invitation is invariably accepted.

True, many of our multi-millionaires are vulgarly extravagant. They are men of coarse and distorted ideas of right, decency, and propriety. Their homes are show-houses for the display of things not worth having. Their garages, stables, and gardens are dedicated to the god of appearances, and not to the comfort of the occupants or their neighbors. They overpay for everything they receive. Superficial people stare at them with eyes of envy, while the sense of the world is sorry for them, and is full of pity for the misguided magnates of wealth, who are no better than plain simpletons, fools, or idiots, mentally incapacitated to perform the proper functions of life, unable to assume any manly part, or else are intentional criminals before the bars of both God and man.

But these rich people at one time practised economy, perhaps the strictest economy; for, if they had not done so, they could not have accumulated sufficient funds to permit them to join the ranks of financial degenerates. They were wise at the start, although the practice of their wisdom gave them greater opportunity to embrace superlative foolishness.

But let not the reader assume that early economy is responsible for later extravagance. The practice of economy cannot be held responsible for its results, which may be bad or may be good, as we choose to make them. The best things of life, including economy and health, can be used to injure ourselves and others.

While a professional man may attain some success without resorting to financial economy, while he may be able to get along without giving much attention to money, or to the saving of it, the business man is doomed to immediate failure, and may never hope to rise above the ranks of insufficient accomplishment, unless he handles his business and personal affairs without extravagance, and systematically and continuously practises every form of legitimate economy. If he does not have the faculty or inclination to do this, he cannot meet with any degree of satisfying success.

I am aware that it is extremely difficult at times for some people to save, but any one can avoid extravagance, if he will.

A man of small income, with a large and growing family, may find it well-nigh impossible to do more than make both ends meet; but, if the right kind of stuff is in him, whatever be his walk in life or his responsibilities, he has no excuse for not trying, for not making every effort to save, even though he may not save anything.

The very determination to save, in itself, coupled with a willingness to make reasonable sacrifices to save, may lead to ultimate success.

What we try to do we may not always do, but what we do not try to do we never do.

The practice of the principle of saving, as much as the value of the amount actually put away, contributes to accomplishment, to safety, to protection, and to probable success.

Nothing impresses a business man more than the ability to save on the part of one who applies for employment. Instinctively the employer has confidence in a saving clerk, and is suspicious of the one who lives up to his means or beyond them. Even though the employer himself is extravagant, he invariably bitterly condemns the employee who copies his foolishness.

Go into any store or office, and line up on one side of the room the men who save and who live properly, and on the other side those who accumulate nothing and who are extravagant, and you will have on one side a line of people of possible success, and on the other side a line of almost certain failure.

Every captain of industry, every millionaire, and every prominent business man will tell you that the beginning of their fortune was founded upon their savings, and that the success they met with was due to the practice of legitimate economy, and to an abhorrence of every kind of extravagance. When they made five dollars a week, they saved at least a small part of it, or they made a most strenuous effort to do so.

Making an effort to do a thing is next to actually doing it.

Every professional man or scientist will positively assert that the beginning of his accomplishment was due to a willingness and an effort, not only to accumulate knowledge, but to properly preserve it, that it might be used when wanted, and none of these men were extravagant along the line of their education or work. They may not have been fortunate in many directions, and may have had little idea of money, but within their laboratories they practised true economy, and seldom tolerated any form of waste.

Every failure in life, if forced to make affidavit on the witness stand, will freely acknowledge, and without qualification, that a lack of proper economy, with or without a superabundance of extravagance, was largely responsible for his downfall.

Let me relate an incident, which came within my own personal experience. A hard-working boy began to save at the age of fourteen. He put away all he could without sacrificing necessary comfort and health. When he was twenty-six he had saved a thousand dollars, was drawing a good salary, and was properly providing for his family. He would have put aside a larger sum had it not been for unavoidable expenses. He had never been extravagant. He was ambitious to go into business for himself in a line which required considerable capital. His thousand dollars would have been but a drop in the bucket of financial necessity. Therefore, he could not hope to start in for himself, unless he could borrow money or obtain a partner with sufficient funds. He was well aware that a partner supplying all of the capital might be unwilling to give him more than an insignificant interest in the business. Not by accident, or because he was lucky, he found a man with less experience and with more money than he had, who wanted to establish himself in this line of trade. This man with some means and less experience was as anxious to find a person of experience as my young friend was to secure a capitalist. My friend with only a thousand dollars borrowed a large sum of his partner, and put all of it into the business, that they might be equal partners with equal capital.

The thousand-dollar man was not really in debt, as debt is commonly considered. Nor did he literally borrow the money wholly on his own responsibility, because all of it went into the business. Of course, he had to pay a fair rate of interest, but that, too, came out of the profits. True, my friend had ability, but the deal was carried through largely because he had saved a thousand dollars. Without that money he might have remained a clerk for many years or for a lifetime. This sum in itself amounted to little, but the fact that he had saved it with necessarily large expenses, and with little opportunity for accumulation, was *prima facie* evidence that he had in him the intrinsic stuff which is a part of the very substance of business success. If he had not shown his capacity for saving, and for saving against obstacles, if he had not been willing to make sacrifices, his experience and ability would not have justified the connection. To-day, he is one of the successful men in his city.

Let me relate another incident, which came also under my personal observation. An acquaintance of mine was a man of considerable ability, cool-headed and energetic. For many years he drew a handsome salary, and at no time was it necessary for his expenses to exceed half of his income. He and his wife lived at the most expensive hotels. He did not save. He was extravagant. Because his income permitted him to have the many things he wanted, he had them. At the age of sixty he found himself without money and without position. He became a burden to his friends, a financial derelict drifting upon the sea of life.

During the forty years of his active business life, when he was receiving more than an average income, he refused to make provision for the future. Before any court of common sense he would have been convicted of criminal extravagance. At sixty he was a broken man, and yet physically and mentally able to do active work.

The position of treasurer in his company was vacant, but the directors discharged him, instead of appointing him to the position. In experience and ability he was able to fill the place. He was popular, and he had been honest and reliable, and there was no black mark against his record. A friend of his at the directors' meeting suggested his name for the position, a place which paid twenty thousand dollars a year. Election seemed probable when the president remarked:

"I am very fond of Mr. Blank. He has been a good man, and has been faithful to our interests. He has more than ordinary capacity, and is able to fill almost any position; but I cannot and will not trust the financial management of this company in the hands of a man who does not know how to handle his own money, who has never saved a dollar, and who has practised every form of extravagance."

The words of the president weighed a ton, and became the mill-stone around this man's neck, which carried him to the bottom. He went down as those have gone down before him, because he had nothing to support him save ability, experience, and faithfulness, a foundation good in itself, but which rests upon the sinking sands of business unless it is propped up by the stones of money; for money is a part of business, and those who cannot keep money, cannot keep business.

Still another incident: A young man lost his position through no fault of his own. He had been receiving two thousand dollars a year, a good salary for one of his age and experience. As he had saved nothing, because of extravagance, it was necessary for him to go to work or starve. Good positions are difficult to find, and a man has to wait a long time, frequently, before he can lucratively locate himself. This young man could not afford to wait; therefore, he was forced to take a subordinate position, and was obliged to work up from the bottom all over again. At the end of five years he was no better off than he had been five years before. If he had not been extravagant, but had saved a little money, which he could have done easily, he would have been able to wait for a better opportunity and would not have lost business caste.

An extravagant man, who loses his position, and who has not saved anything, is at a tremeudous disadvantage. He must get to work immediately, and is usually obliged to take what he can find. He cannot hold his position in the business world and wait for the right opportunity. His vulnerable parts are exposed. The world knows that he is out of a job, and because he is obliged to take an inferior one, it assumes that he lost his last position through his own fault. He goes down, because he has nothing to hold him up, and misses success.

I think that I may say truly that success is due

to distinct and willing sacrifices, to the doing away with every form of extravagance, to the systematic saving of money, to the gaining and preservation of knowledge, and to integrity and honesty.

Don't imagine, young man, or man of any age, that the possession of automobile or motor-boat gives you even the tiniest boost into any kind of society strong enough to stand the faintest zephyr of the gentlest breeze. Society worth while is built of stronger stuff than that represented purely by the expenditure of money. And don't get into your head, or if you do, get it out with the greatest despatch, that your credit at the bank, at the grocer's and the market, or anywhere else, has gone up a cent because of an automobile or a motor-boat or anything else of that class. The chances are that your credit has gone down several dollars, especially at your bank. Fully sixty per cent of all purchasers of motors for land or water cannot afford the luxury, and one-half of this sixty per cent have either mortgaged their real estate, if they had any, or made some other unjustifiable sacrifice, that they may travel in style. The names of a proportion, and perhaps a large one, of automobile riders are to be found in the mortgage department of the registry of deeds.

The purchase of anything one cannot easily

afford, if it is to be seen, as is an automobile or a motor-boat, works against the financial credit of the owner, and does not give him any reputation except that of being extravagant. If he can enjoy what he cannot afford, well and good for him. If he can be happy in a motor-car which represents a mortgage on his house or the cashing of a life insurance policy to the lessening of the protection due himself and family,— again, I say, well and good for him. He is an undesirable citizen, unfit to be a husband and father, untrustworthy, unreliable, and unrespected.

The smile of extravagance never was put on to stay. The day of reckoning is sure to dawn dark and stormy. There is only one result, and that is financial embarrassment with or without the wreck of prospects, reputation, and family. Every extravagance (everything is an extravagance if it cannot be afforded) has to be paid for, and if it is not paid for by money which can be spared, the settlement is made sooner or later, and usually sooner, at an expense which makes the usurer's interest seem small in comparison.

I am not asking any one to give up all the comforts of life, or to place himself on the rack of business, or to live continuously in a windowless laboratory of science, never to look up to the blue sky or down at the green grass, for every one has a right to rest, comfort, light, and sunshine. These things all contribute to the spiritual upbuilding of man. But he who will not sacrifice extravagance and luxury for better things, will never realize any laudable ambition, assuming that such a man can have one.

Every accomplishment is born in travail. Without pain nothing has ever been done. Sacrifice accomplishes every attainment. The men on top are those who worked the hardest at the bottom. The most skilful wielder of the sword has successfully carried the gun.

The practice of economy stands for success, although none of its practitioners may ever rise above the common level.

The practice of extravagance leads to ultimate and certain failure.

By economy we may succeed; by extravagance we surely fail.

CHAPTER VII

PETTY EXTRAVAGANCES

EVERY cent is worth a cent, and every dollar represents one hundred cents.

Take care of the cents, and the dollars will take care of themselves.

Half of the waste of the world is below the dollar mark.

Many a man loses many dollars, a cent at a time.

Small or petty extravagances, the promiscuous or careless spending of a few cents, lead up to losses of every size.

One who does not keep an account, and enter every out-going cent, can have no conception of the leaks, which in time are large enough to flood him with disaster.

A cent, or a nickel, or a dime, is small in itself, but large in the aggregate.

Most spendthrifts have some appreciation of large sums, and many of them do not throw away money in the bulk, but limit their extravagances to the constant expenditure of pennies, nickels, dimes, and dollars, yet fail to understand the reason why they are always short of money, and why they are never able to get ahead.

Petty Extravagances

A careful scrutiny of the lives of successful men will discover that most of them were economical in small things, and weighed every cent.

Practically all accumulations of money began with small savings, with an appreciation of the value of a cent.

Of course, this may be carried too far, and is, perhaps, partly responsible for the meanness of men of wealth, who seem more willing to pay five thousand dollars for an automobile than to give five cents extra for a hair-cut. But, although this petty saving may be the foundation of continuous closeness and meanness, without it success is impossible, and a competence can never be realized.

There is a vast gulf between the miser and the careful saver. The former hoards for the sake of keeping the money, and the latter saves for the sake of principle, and for protection.

The conscientious saver may even approach meanness, but better that than the opposite, for the mean man is seldom a public charge; if he does nothing else, he is able to take care of himself.

The strenuous life we are living, and the continuous display, offer every opportunity for extravagance, and place temptation upon every corner. One must brace oneself against it or fall.

There are a thousand petty extravagances, each

by itself amounting to little, but altogether producing a disastrous total.

Take the soda water and pop beer fad, for example. There is not a hamlet large enough for a post-office, without one or more soft-drink counters, which are responsible for a habit having much to do with the careless expenditure of nickels.

In the first place, the drinking of soft drinks is precarious; many of them are neither cooling nor healthful. Although they may not be injurious, they are usually over-sweetened, and may be impure. They do not quench the thirst, but, instead, stimulate the thirst for another drink. So far as I know, not one of them contains any medicinal or tonic property. Their value appears to be largely limited to the advertisements of them. Plain water is always procurable, and few of us drink half enough of it. Water is Nature's own and best thirst-quencher, and is usually free.

Hundreds of thousands of young men and women average twenty cents a day for soft drinks during the summer. It is a fact that the majority of soda, root beer, and tonic drinkers are those who cannot afford the nickels, and it is also a fact that the majority of well-to-do people are not regular patrons of soft-drink bars. If you do not believe this, stand in front of a soda-water counter and size up the drinkers. You will find that most of them have small incomes, are clerks and shop-girls, and others to whom five cents is quite a sum of money.

Bear in mind that I am talking of averages, not exceptions. Comparatively few of us are soft-drink abstainers, but the better class of us are not soft-drink drunkards.

The next time you have your shoes shined by a professional boot-black, carefully observe the appearance and probable financial condition of the patrons of the boot-black booth. A large proportion of them are shabbily dressed, and many of them wear shoes not worth a shine. True, many a well-to-do person is obliged to use the public blacking-stand, because no one is supposed to carry a box of shoe-blacking with him, or a polishing brush; but I am referring to the habitual patron, who deliberately leaves his home with his shoes unpolished and stops at the nearest blacking booth. This he does every day at an expense of thirty-five cents a week. A box of the best shoe-polish costs ten cents, and there are, at least, fifty shines in a box. Fifty self-shines, then, cost ten cents, and fifty shoe-stand shines cost two dollars and fifty cents. Furthermore, a self-shine takes half of the time required for a boot-black shine, and time is, or should be, money.

Then there is the shaving proposition. A first-class shave costs from ten to twenty cents, a self-shave costs less than a cent. The self-shaver can shave in half the time occupied by the barber.

Figure it out for yourself,— one cent a shave, or seven cents a week, or, say, fifteen cents a shave or one dollar and five cents a week. It is a fact that comparatively few men of standing, character, and intelligence patronize a barber, except for a hair-cut. Most of these men are self-shavers, and many of them, who can afford to patronize the barber-shop, shave themselves because of the amount saved and the cleanliness of the operation. Very few cannot shave themselves, even if they think that they cannot. I doubt, however, if there is any man of any intelligence, who cannot use a safety razor.

Perhaps dress, more than anything else, is responsible for large and small extravagances, especially by those of small incomes.

It has been said that the average employer pays less for his clothes than the average employee does, and that the majority of well-to-do people, barring the newly rich and the snob, are more economical in dress than are those of small incomes, who seem to think that the man is known by the clothes he wears, and that they, therefore, are known by the clothes they should not wear.

I have considered dress in another chapter, but

in passing, let me say that the average person expends double the amount necessary for plain, simple, and appropriate clothes, and that a part of this waste is for the purchase of so-called trimmings, which seldom improve the appearance of the wearer.

The car-riding habit is another source of petty extravagance. Thousands of people ride instead of saving money and aiding health by walking. A rain-coat, a pair of water-proof shoes or rubber boots, and an umbrella or rain-shedding hat, are money-savers and health-makers. Unless you are physically unable to walk, walk all you can, walk for the sake of your health and for the saving of money.

I am not asking any one to live in a hermit's house, for I believe in entertainment. The good theatre is an educational institution, but the theatre habit is responsible for a proportion of our extravagances. Theatre-going has a tail to it, the cost of the ticket being but a part of it. It is often connected with ice cream and suppers, or boxes of candy, and calls for additional clothes. In every large city there are maintained stock company play-houses, where the best of plays, well acted, are presented twice daily, and the prices are low. Many a student of the drama considers these theatres far more educational and beneficial than are those devoted to bright stars, shining in a firmament of supporting darkness. They may not properly represent the playwright, because the star usually takes the bulk of the money, and the company may be hired like cattle. The price of a good seat in an expensive theatre will cover the cost of four good ones in the stock company play-house. I am not, however, asking you never to see a great play acted by a brilliant star, but you do not need to see half as many of them as you think you do. Theatre money is not absolutely essential, and there should not be theatre money to the exclusion of money for real necessities.

The dining-out tendency is to be deplored. It costs many times more than it is worth. The expensive dinner is not nutritious. It is the forerunner of dissipation. It leads to every form of extravagance. Do not deceive yourself into believing that your presence in a fashionable *café* helps you into society, for it has no tendency that way. It is the other way. The man you work for has no respect for you, because he knows you cannot afford to dine in expensive places. He looks upon you as a fool, because you are a fool. Turtle soup and terrapin, champagne and mixed drinks, are never near the door which opens into good society. The show-off dinner shows you off in a way you do not realize. I am not referring to an occasional evening at a restaurant or hotel, where good food is served at reasonable prices, because the stomach, as well as the mind, needs an occasional change; but extravagant eating is doubly extravagant when it affects both the health and the pocket-book.

Smoking has become so general, and is practised by so many high-grade people, that the subject is very difficult to approach without giving the appearance of prejudice. The statement may be made, however, that ninety per cent of habitual smokers would, if placed under oath, say that they wished they had never begun the habit. There are two kinds of smokers, the extravagant smoker, and the one who does not expend much money for his tobacco.

Whether or not smoking is to be condemned is a question which each one must settle for himself, but extravagant or excessive smoking is without excuse. Not one smoker in a million can tell the difference between a good cigar and the very expensive one. He buys his cigars by price, not to suit his taste. There is very little reason for smoking a cigar which retails for more than ten cents. The quality of cigars above this price is largely confined to the name.

If you are bound to smoke, cultivate the pipe habit,— a good pipe costs very little,— and first-class tobacco is not expensive. You are not likely to smoke as much with a pipe as with a cigar. The healthiest pipe to use is one that is absorbent, like the old-fashioned corn-cob, which costs five cents or less, and which may be thrown away every few days.

It is a significant fact that a proportion, and, perhaps, a large one, of professional men and brain-workers who smoke, prefer the pipe to the cigar. Then, smoking a pipe eliminates treating, and treating is responsible for part of the expense of cigar smoking.

If you ask me for advice about smoking, I would say do not smoke; but if you will smoke anyway, cultivate the pipe habit, unless you are financially able to smoke good cigars without feeling the cost.

Gum chewing is another petty extravagance. There is absolutely no excuse for it. It does not, I believe, contribute one dot to good digestion or health. I do not think that a reputable physician would recommend it. True, it may not do any harm; but it is an expensive habit and one which is very disagreeable to others. It certainly cheapens the person who does it.

Habitual candy eating is not only injurious to health, but it is an extravagance without excuse. A moderate amount of good candy does not injure the digestion and is a source of satisfaction, and I would not bar it out, but the eating of candy, as it is usually taken, is absolutely injurious and altogether too expensive to be justifiable.

Trying to make a show,— I have spoken of this in other chapters,— is one of the greatest menaces to sense and economy. It accomplishes nothing, except to make a fool of its practitioner. It makes no difference whether it is confined to the multi-millionaire, to the merchant, to the housewife, or to the shop-girl, it is the personification of vulgarity and social idiocy. It stands for everything low and contemptible. It is responsible for much extravagance, and never gives any one a position in any society, no, not even in the lowest, for the show-man or the show-woman, bedecked with real or paste diamonds, has no respect for others of his or her kind.

The desire to wear jewelry of any kind, especially expensive jewelry, could not exist in true civilization.

I know that I am treading upon dangerous ground, because some men, and most women, say that they love jewelry for art's sake, and believe that their admiration is genuine. I will speak of it here only as it affects the moderate pocket-book. The idea that diamonds, and other expensive self-decorations, are good investments is based upon a wrong standard.

The love of expensive jewelry has impoverished

many a woman, yes, and has done worse for her. Many a beautiful hand has become unattractive because of the too many rings worn upon its fingers. Many a poor clerk has purchased a watch altogether too expensive for him. The money has gone into the case, not into the works. Thousands of young men have gone without proper underclothing that they might accumulate sufficient money to buy a hundred-dollar ring for a ten-dollar girl.

Right here may I not speak of the bride's trousseau, which usually costs three times more than the bride's parents can afford? The very principle of it is wrong. It enables the wife to begin in extravagance. It sets the wrong pace at the start.

Expensive wedding tours, by those who can hardly afford local car-fare, frequently leave a mark which is never eradicated.

In closing this important chapter let me not leave the reader with the impression that I would take from him many of the little pleasures of life, those inexpensive things which cast a glow upon our everyday gloom, and which make for individual and general happiness. I have simply attempted to warn him against any expenditure that he cannot afford, and to show him that the music of true economy and genuine happiness never comes from the jingling of coin.

CHAPTER VIII

DRESS

IN the chapter entitled "Petty Extravagances" I have spoken of dress, but it seems advisable to consider it by itself, for extravagant and inappropriate dressing is very close to the principal source of failure.

I am not asking any man to dress habitually in khaki clothes, or any woman to wear continually burlaps and calico, although I must admit that if this were a common custom, most of us would be happier, healthier, and better.

The habit of adorning the body appears to have started with the pre-historic savage. The first thing he did, after he knew enough to do anything, was to decorate his body, either with paint or clothes. This continued in various stages until commercialism was placed upon the throne, and business, always selfish and shrewd, saw in dress its most magnificent money-making opportunity. It found willing devotees.

To-day a large proportion of the manufacturing and retail business of the world is confined to the making and selling of outer clothes. Fully one-half of the advertisements, which appear in the daily newspapers, and one-quarter of those in the magazines, exploit the outer garments of men and women and those things which stand for appearance and show, and not for comfort and necessity.

At a recent World's Exposition, the authorities found it necessary to place special police surveillance around an exhibition of fashion, which protection was not needed for any other exhibit on the grounds.

Crowds are seldom found in front of the show-window presenting necessary underwear, or clothes for service and comfort; but are found gazing at the commercial display of hats and expensive outer garments, which are intended to adorn both men and women, especially the latter.

The tendency, and I may say, the almost insane desire to look well on the outside, or to look better than our neighbors, is responsible for about half of all extravagance, and for hundreds of thousands of failures.

The criterion of dress is not appropriateness, but a show of expense. It has little to do with comfort or with attractiveness. To dress as well as, or better than, our neighbors, is a deplorable ambition, which insures failure, and which is responsible for over-work, the extravagance of over-dressing, and the inappropriate decoration of our outsides, from our bodies to our houses. It is without excuse, and is often criminally wrong, and the cause of half of our downfalls.

In the first place, it is foolish, because it does not accomplish anything. The over-dressed person has no respect for one of her kind. The most extravagantly dressed people cannot cover up the size of their incomes. Folk know what they are worth, whether or not they buy their clothes for cash or on instalments, whether or not they pay their bills, whether or not they can afford to dress as they do. If they over-dress, or dress beyond their means, the people they intend to impress look upon them with scorn, although half of these folk may be as foolish and do the same thing.

It is a fact that the best people, and often the richest people, dress the simplest, although it is unfortunately true that some multi-millionaires are shoddy in appearance and make as vulgar displays of their money as do the genuinely shoddy.

Decent people, intelligent people, and well-to-do people are not addicted to vulgar or extravagant display. Expensive clothes, worn especially by those of moderate means, are vulgar and show lack of character and dishonesty on the part of the wearer.

Over-dressing to-day is often the cause of poverty to-morrow.

Unless your income is large, you cannot have expensive clothes, in justice to yourself, your family, your business, and your future.

If you would save money, protect yourself, and command the respect of truly respectable men and women, dress within your means, dress moderately and inexpensively, and remember that the clothes which look well need not be those which cost the most.

Any attempt on your part to dress beyond your means, or to use yourself as a frame for the display of fashion, reacts against you and does not pay when viewed from any standpoint.

This subject is again spoken of in the chapters entitled "Extravagance," "Living Beyond Our Means," and "Petty Extravagances."

CHAPTER IX

TAKING ADVICE

IN the unabridged catalogue of everyday life, probably nothing occupies a more conspicuous or voluminous space than that of advice-asking with or without advice-taking, particularly by would-be investors, and others, who have small sums of money waiting for proper placing.

It has been said that something-for-nothing is worth just what is paid for it,—nothing,—and that free advice belongs to the something-for-nothing class. As a matter of fact, this popular notion or estimate of the value of advice is far removed from truth.

Advice is one of the greatest of business and social commodities.

To condemn advice, as a whole, because there is much bad advice in circulation, is as foolish as it would be to object to bread-eating because some bread is sour.

Only the fool is sufficient unto himself. The wise and successful man never settles an important question by himself alone, whether the matter be of investment or of other purport. His accomplishments are due to his composite qualities,— to his ability to combine what he knows with what others know. He reserves for himself the right to throw the casting vote, but he never does it until he has sifted conditions through the minds of others.

It is axiomatic that anything more than ordinary success is due to inclusiveness,— to the ability to know what others know, or rather, to use what others know.

Do not misunderstand me. I do not mean to say that the man of success does not think for himself. He does. The volume of his self-thinking is proportionate to that of his action and to the extent of the profitable result.

From every standpoint,— from that of policy, selfishness, and safety,— advice should be sought and followed, to some extent, at least, provided intelligence is in evidence at every stage.

In these rapid and strenuous times, things have become specialized, and are managed by specialists,— too much so, I think, because it has forced the all-round man out of business. But so long as this condition maintains, we, too, must specialize to a greater extent than was necessary long ago, and we must know one thing much better than all others, and realize that others know other things better than we do.

While none of us are infallible and while

error is inevitable, the advice of an honest, conservative, successful banker is worth more to the would-be investor, than is the composite opinion of a hundred college presidents,— you may multiply the number of college presidents, if you will.

The lawyer may be conscientious, and so may be the minister, but if they know the practice of their professions as they should know it, there is every reason why they would be poor and inaccurate weighers of financial things.

I am speaking, of course, upon general principles, because many professional men are good financiers, but professional men are, as a rule, incompetent to travel very far from theoretical fields.

Experience counts for as much as ability does, and men out of business, whatever may be their natural abilities, are too far from business to manipulate business.

No small investor, or investor of any size, for that matter, should place his money in any direction without obtaining advice from two or more persons competent to weigh financial values.

Let us suppose, for example, that a young man can save twenty-five dollars a month. This twenty-five dollars, small as it is, is more to him than are twenty-five thousand dollars to a man of extensive property. It is his duty to place it at the minimum of risk, to secure for it the maximum of security. He cannot afford to speculate. Much as he desires a high rate of interest, he should not take the chances which usually accompany large profits. He hears of a certain opportunity, which may be industrial stock. Even though he may be acquainted with the concern, and personally know all of its officials, he should thoroughly investigate what is back of the stock, refusing to allow his own opinion to count if it cannot be substantiated by the opinion of others. The easiest and best way for him to go at it, is to consult with conservative and able men, who are in a position to know whether or not this stock is worth buying. He should not depend upon the advice of any one man, no matter how reliable that man may be. We are all subject to bias, and many a man who is fair up to his light, may be the unfairest of all. We are children, or men, of circumstances; we cannot follow, with safety, the road staked out by ourselves, or by any one individual. No one man ever made a chart safe to steer by. No one man by himself ever constructed an engine that was worth the cost of setting up. No one man ever did anything, or knew anything, wholly by himself alone. There is no such thing as individual originality in its absolutely pure state. Success is due to adding to the little we know, the much that others know. Safety is vested in the composite.

If the men visited by the young man do not know anything about investments, they can refer him, undoubtedly, to others who do know if the investment is worth while. If he cannot find at least two reliable and conservative men, who have no interest in the stock mentioned, to advise him to purchase it, he had better let it severely alone.

I think one may establish an invariable rule, subject to no exception, that stock, or any other form of security, is not reasonably safe, unless it is unqualifiedly recommended by as many as two honest and conservative business men familiar with investment matters.

In the interest of safety, I would advise the small investor to keep away from any form of investment, even if a dozen business men recommend it, if two or three equally good business men condemn it.

The man with a small income had better lean, and lean heavily, towards the side of over-carefulness.

Most emphatically would I advise the small investor to place no dependence whatever in any statement made by any person interested in the stock for sale, unless such claim is too reasonable to admit of suspicion, or is backed up and endorsed by outsiders.

There are three kinds of investments, the risky, the reasonably safe, and what may be considered, commercially, as absolutely safe. Of course, nothing is absolute, but I will not change the word. The small investor, the wage-earner, and salary-receiver have no business to consider other than the last. This class of investment has the support of conservative and able business men and financiers. The thing of unknown value is not likely to have much value. It is pretty hard to keep a good thing down, and an investment worth while is not kept under a business bushel, but the light of it shines to the world.

The best advisers upon investments are, as a rule, presidents and other high officials, representing banks and banking houses. They are not speculators, they hold their positions on account of their conservatism and extreme caution. They are not interested in other than clean and safe securities. They are not likely to be biassed. But I would not advise the small investor to trust any one of them implicitly, because that particular one may be prejudiced from self-interest, or from other motives, and no one is infallible. It is better, therefore, to seek the advice of several of these men. If they agree, he may feel safe. If they do not, he had better consider something else.

Advice then, if it is of the right kind, is of importance, and of vital consequence. To refuse to ask it, or accept it, shows pronounced pigheadedness and a tremendous lack of reliability.

Ninety per cent of all the losses which have fallen upon small investors, would not have occurred if they had obtained good advice and followed it.

All of our mistakes and losses are not due, necessarily, to personal inability or ignorance, but to that sort of unheroic daring which seems to order us to do what we please, to enter a blind pool with eyes covered and with ears closed.

He who knows it all, knows nothing. He who knows how little he knows, knows much. The individual is weak, the composite is strong.

CHAPTER X

LOANING TO FRIENDS

I WOULD not adulterate, by even a microscopic drop, the milk of human kindness. We should help each other, for the more we help each other, the more we help ourselves. Reciprocity is one of the great elements of success; without it nothing is possible, save the product of selfishness, and the results of selfishness and avarice should have no place in human affairs.

Things, at their best, are hard to bear, and most of us are straining our bodies and minds. Perfection and certainty do not exist in this world. If we would do anything, we must willingly take reasonable chances. To do otherwise, is to do nothing.

Many a man obtained his profitable start in life through the kindness of a friend, who loaned him money, or in some other way assisted him at a critical period in his career, and so enabled him to carry his load over a dead centre.

No man with a heart in him, or with a normal amount of sense, would condemn the loaning of money to friends, or would he make any other rigid rule against helping others. The establishment of such a law would bolt the life out of love,— would lower us below the animal, for even the beast is generous. Here, as in all else, judgment must be exercised. It is better to be generous than to practise the opposite, but it is far better to be fair to yourself, as well as to others, always remembering that true generosity considers the giver as well as the receiver.

But the promiscuous loaning of money to friends, who are financially embarrassed, is precarious, unfair, and ungenerous, and is as likely to injure the receiver as the giver. It is not a financial investment, and should not be so considered. It is an accommodation, a thing of kindness, a thing to be done, or not to be done, as conditions justify. In making the decision, do not allow your generosity to get the better of your judgment, or your judgment to selfishly influence your generosity.

Your friend comes to you to borrow one hundred dollars. You must consider, first, whether or not you can afford to *give* him the money, whether or not you can take the ordinary or extraordinary chance in justice to yourself and your family. If you decide that you cannot afford to do this, then you should not loan the money. The security you have may be limited to the good intention of the borrower. If you can loan this money, or rather, if you can afford to give it, and the borrower is deserving, by all means accommodate him. If, on the other hand, the borrower is not deserving, refuse him whether or not you can stand the loss. If he is deserving, then it is a question of how great a sacrifice you must make to accommodate him. At times you would be justified in making a great sacrifice. At other times any sacrifice would be wrong.

It is undoubtedly true that the majority of financially embarrassed people do not deserve consideration. They are in their present deplorable condition because they were unwilling to save, and refused to make reasonable sacrifices, and, as a rule, they are without good judgment and have little moral stamina. They would rather borrow than make any effort to earn. They would rather do what amounts to stealing than to save money. They would work harder to borrow a dollar than they would labor to earn two dollars. They are willing that their friends should take the chances. They would pay their bills if it were convenient for them to do so, but they would make no effort to meet an obligation. These men deserve no assistance, and only morbid sentiment would suggest that any one help them, unless the aid goes to innocent members of their families, who would suffer hard privation if outside aid was not forthcoming.

One would be justified in helping even the spendthrift, if his family cannot be assisted in any other way. The loan, then, is to the family, not to the head member of it.

There is a class of borrower, who is in desperate straits through no fault of his own. He is thoroughly honest and deserves to be considered. He is a hard worker, would save if he could, and is not extravagant. He intends, always, to return the money he has borrowed; he will make any sacrifice to do so. This man is deserving of assistance, and the lender is justified in aiding him, provided he can do so without undue sacrifice; and sometimes he should make even more than ordinary sacrifice for his friend in trouble.

Here is where human kindness comes in. Here is where we are justified in sacrificing ourselves for our friends. The man who will not do this, unless it causes hardships which he has no right to sustain, is unmanly, ungenerous, and a poor citizen.

Another class of borrowers would obtain money for business purposes,—not because they are financially embarrassed, but because they desire to increase their business or to do something else equally legitimate. But the man of small income should not consider them as investment propositions, even though they offer an exorbitant rate of interest. These men, if thoroughly honest and reliable, can obtain money from the bank, or from professional money-lenders, or by furnishing business or other security, which may be acceptable to those who can afford to take speculative chances.

In loaning money, as well as in doing anything else, one should consider oneself as much as one considers the borrower. It is unfair and wrong for a man of responsibility and family to throw his money at the fellow who is down, unless he feels that it is his duty to do so, or, that by so doing, he will aid the innocent and dependent, or is reasonably sure that he will get his money back.

Most men, who have eaten both the bread and pie of life, and have taken no thought of to-morrow, expect the man who has earned the right to eat pie, by getting along without it, to share both the bread and pie with the fellow who does not deserve either.

To sum up:— The small investor, or the man of moderate income, should never loan money as an investment without security. If he wants to help a friend, he should place his friend's necessities and his own side by side. If his friend deserves help, or his family are in need, it is justifiable to lend him the money, provided the lender can afford to give it, or is able to sustain the loss.

This loaning of money is often a question of friendship, and is not usually a business proposition. It should never be done thoughtlessly or upon the spur of the moment. The would-be borrower and the lender should talk the matter over, each should be frank with the other, and aid should be given when it is deserved and the helper can afford to help.

CHAPTER XI

TAKING SPECULATIVE CHANCES

THE speculator is nothing more nor less than a financial gambler, although all speculation is not necessarily dishonest. But, nevertheless, the element of chance must accompany all speculation, and is not limited, by any means, to purely speculative manipulators. Opportunity for risk and chance is a part of the making of success, and accompanies all business-doing.

There is nothing sure in this world, in business or out of it, and some risk must be taken by everybody who would accomplish anything.

There is right speculation and wrong speculation; the difference is somewhat a question of degree; and it is extremely difficult to trace, definitely, the line between what seems to be preeminently right and what would appear to be essentially wrong.

Commercially speaking, the speculator is not a doer of regular business; he does not obtain standard goods that he may sell them at a profit; he deals more in chances and takes large risks; and he succeeds, if the price he receives is larger, on an average, than the price he pays. In the transaction of his business the element of chance is more than normal, and there is a larger opportunity for loss, and a greater one for unusual profit, than would be likely to occur in the buying and selling of ordinary commodities.

Whether or not speculation, as it is commonly defined, is right or wrong from the standpoint of the moralist, no man of small income has a moral or business right to take so-called speculative chances,— to place himself in a position where there is more than common risk. To do so is unfair to himself and to his family, and is pretty sure to result in complete financial breakdown.

Speculation is for those who make a business of it,— who are willing to play the game to win or to lose, and who are financially able to sustain loss, looking at it as inevitable, as a natural consequence of speculation, feeling that the balance-sheet at the end of the year will show some profit, but all the time recognizing the possibility of complete failure.

These men train themselves for their work, they make a business of taking chances. Some of them succeed; most of them fail in the end. But even if they all succeeded, their success would not justify any one outside of their kind in taking speculative chances.

While the trained speculator may win, he who

does not understand speculation, who is not keyed up to it, is absolutely sure of failure. Probably the love of speculation is, with extravagance, responsible for ninety per cent of loss.

Keep out of speculation. Refuse to take the maximum risk, or even more than the minimum risk, unless you are trained in the work and can meet disaster as calmly as you would success; and remember that, if you are a married man, your willingness to take speculative chances cannot be taken as an excuse for any action which is likely to bring suffering upon your family.

It is questionable whether or not you have a right to injure yourself, but no one will justify you in doing anything which causes the innocent to suffer with you.

Being fair to yourself is not enough. You must be fair to those dependent upon you.

You cannot be sure, but you can be reasonably so, and anything less than the reasonable is wrong.

CHAPTER XII

THE SAVINGS BANK

THE savings bank, or, as it is sometimes called, the institution for savings, is a repository for money, authorized by, and organized under, special State banking laws, and it is not under the jurisdiction of the Federal Government.

Many of the States have enacted and execute the most strenuous regulations, which place their savings banks under the strictest supervision, compelling them to conduct their business, and particularly the investment side of it, in the most conservative manner, that the risk of failure or loss may be reduced to the minimum.

These banking laws, when consistently complied with,— and to the credit of the savings bank fraternity it may be said that few depart from them, — do not permit the bank to invest the depositors' money except for the purchase of the highest grade of bonds, for the loaning of money on mortgages of the better class, and in the ownership of real estate. In the States where the laws are particularly strict, the bank can purchase only preferred bonds and other high-grade securities, and is not permitted to loan upon real estate more than sixty per cent of the assessed or real valuation.

Most of the States have done all that they possibly can do to safeguard the depositors' money, the legislatures realizing that the failure of a savings bank means loss to the people who can least afford to lose.

The savings bank, then, becomes a public charge, and offers every reason for every kind of legislative safeguard.

The savings bank is governed or managed by a board of trustees, no member of which is allowed to receive any salary or emolument for his services. The board elects a president, who usually draws no salary, but who may do so if he is active in the management of the bank; and a treasurer, who acts as executive officer, and who appoints the necessary clerks and assistants, none of whom are paid more than reasonable salaries, except in some places where the laws are not strictly enforced and the management is neither conservative nor economical.

The good savings bank is, in reality, a philanthropic institution, under the management of the strongest, most conservative, must reliable and highest grade of men in the community, who voluntarily give their services for the benefit of the people, and because the position of trustee is a highly honorable one.

Other savings banks, legally operated in some States, while depositories for money, and while they render, apparently, the same service to depositors, are money-making institutions, established and maintained for the benefit of the stockholders. They are usually connected with trust companies, and are conducted as separate departments. They are not, as a rule, as conservatively managed, or as safe, as are the regular mutual savings banks, which are not supposed to be money-makers.

All savings banks are subject to State inspection, the severity of which is dependent upon the strenuosity of the laws controlling the banks.

The large majority of savings banks are financially sound, conservative, economical, and carefully managed, and their depositors may be assured of what is very close to absolute security. But there are scattered throughout the country quite a number of small and badly managed banks, usually controlled by one man, or a combination of men, who run the banks for their own profit, and who loan the money, either to themselves indirectly, or to others who are in league with them. In outward appearance, these banks may show every indication of solidity, and only careful investigation will locate their weakness. They are continuously failing, and sometimes the depositor loses all his money; but usually he receives from fifty to seventy-five per cent of his deposit. Many of these banks offer more than the current rate of interest, using it as a bait to attract the depositor.

It is possible that a well-managed savings bank, under certain local conditions, can pay as much as five per cent, but no conservative business man would recommend such a bank, unless he was thoroughly familiar with all that is going on inside of it.

Upon general principles, I would not advise any one to deposit money in any savings bank paying more than four per cent. Money is worth less to-day than it used to be; and because money is cheap, interest is low. Loans are frequently made at three per cent, and some bonds do not pay more than two per cent net. Good four per cent bonds yield less than four per cent, unless they are purchased at par.

The first-class savings bank cannot, and will not, loan its money except on gilt-edged securities, nor will it purchase any questionable security, or anything of speculative value. Consequently, it cannot easily obtain more than five per cent net on its investments, that is to say, its money cannot possibly earn more than five per cent, on an average, and it is likely to earn less. From these earnings must be subtracted the expense of running the bank.

It is obvious, then, that no conservatively managed institution for savings can afford to pay its depositors much more than four per cent, although it may occasionally be permitted to give an extra dividend.

Beware, then, of the bank paying more than a normal rate of interest, which should not be far from four per cent.

It is well to give your local bank the preference, but do not do so unless you are sure of its reliability and strength. Most savings banks receive deposits by mail, and I would advise the use of banks located in States where the banking laws are strictly maintained, unless the local bank has a reputation too high to be questioned. A few banks will not receive deposits from those outside of their territory, but the majority of them do not make this restriction.

The frequent failure of savings banks has naturally prejudiced many people against them, but this prejudice is unfair to the savings banks in general. Practically all of the failures are confined to small institutions and to those managed by incompetent or dishonest men. Occasionally a small bank goes to pieces on account of defalcation, because the business done by it is not large enough to sustain a considerable loss.

Defalcation on the part of the bank officials is always possible. No law, or regulation, or inspection, can completely guard against it. There is always opportunity for theft. Nor is it possible for any one to know whether or not a trusted official will fall. Many an honest man, under severe temptation, may use the money of the bank for speculation, with a genuine intention of returning it. He fails, as most speculators do, and, consequently, cannot return the money. If the bank is small, the whole, or a part, of the money comes out of the depositors.

It may seem hardly fair for me to discriminate against the small bank, because many of them are as solid as the Rock of Gibraltar, and most of them are managed by men whose integrity is far above par. But it is, nevertheless, true that while human nature is weak, defalcation is always possible, and the robbing of a small bank usually wrecks the bank, while the same amount of money taken from a large institution would not affect the depositors. It is always possible for the treasurer, or other official, of a small bank, to make false entries, and to cover up his dishonesty for an almost indefinite period, and, as he largely controls the finances of the bank, he can easily wreck it; while no one official has the same opportunity in a larger bank. At most, he can steal but a small sum compared with the total amount of deposits. A defalcation of fifty thousand or one hundred thousand dollars may ruin a small savings bank, while a theft of the same size would not affect a large bank. Then, frequently, trustees do not exercise their prerogative, but leave everything to the treasurer. This gives him the opportunity for embezzlement.

The large bank, on the other hand, is officered by many officials, and no one of them can get hold of much of the money without the knowledge and consent of others.

As I have already said, there are several small banks run wholly in the interest of their trustees or officers, and although none of these men may be direct defaulters or embezzlers, they loan the bank's money, either to themselves directly, or to men they are connected with, often taking unfair and even criminal risks. Sooner or later the bank will go down.

Comparatively few large banks have failed, and few of them have been affected by defalcation or by occasional bad investments. They are large enough to stand a loss of reasonable size and they can sustain one many times larger than that which would wreck a small bank.

I would advise no one to place money in any savings bank, except in those of national reputation, until he has investigated the standing of the bank by making the most searching inquiries of local bankers and reliable business men; and I would further advise him to give the large bank the preference, upon general principles.

If his local bank is small, and if it is not managed and officered by honest local business men, I would advise him to deposit his money in some larger savings bank, located elsewhere.

An officer of any national bank, or any bank president, or the leading financier of the town, can give him all the information he desires.

It is well to inquire of more than one, for many an honest man is biassed by special interests.

If one would be on the safest side, it would be well for him to make inquiries outside of his town, addressing them to the officials of some national bank or savings bank of extensive reputation.

The fact that there are two or more thoroughly good men on the board of trustees may not be taken as evidence that the bank is sound, unless these men take an active interest in the bank's business. Many a good man allows himself to be elected a trustee, and gives no attention to his duties. Frequently he is placed upon the board wholly for the use of his name. His connection with the bank, then, has little significance, and does not add to the bank's value.

Persistent and careful inquiry will enable any one to get pretty close to the true condition of the bank.

Better go too far with your inquiries than to do otherwise.

Never deposit in any bank which is not well spoken of and which is not supported by the careful and conservative business men in the town.

The savings bank is obliged to make an annual statement, and this statement is likely to be technically true; but it is not, as a rule, intelligible to other than experts. Most reports read well upon their faces. Unless you are familiar with financial matters, do not allow this report to influence you for or against the bank, until you have shown it to some one who understands it. Be suspicious of the bank which places its office furniture among its assets, and which shows other weak collateral. Keep away from the bank which lends more than sixty per cent of the real value of the property mortgaged. But if you are not able to weigh financial values, you will have to depend largely upon the standing and reputation of your advisers. If they are men of character and high financial standing, and are not speculators, you are not likely to go far from right in taking their advice.

The savings bank is certainly the most convenient depository for savings. Its depositors may have their money back when they want it, although the bank may require from thirty to ninety days' notice of withdrawal of the entire deposit. This condition is seldom taken advantage of by other than weak or small banking institutions. The first-class and larger savings banks invariably waive this condition, and pay in full when requested, except in cases of a run on the bank, and even then most sound banks do not refuse to give the depositor his money when he asks for it.

The owner of mortgages, stocks, bonds, and real estate, although his money may be securely invested, may not be able to unload, so to speak, — to obtain his cash without a long delay,— and, therefore, he may have to pay something to somebody, usually a broker, for the privilege of obtaining his money. The savings bank deposit is, on the other hand, available cash, and is, further, interest-earning cash.

The fact that one can get his money when he wants it from the savings bank may operate against this form of deposit for those who have an almost criminal desire to use their available money. For this reason, it may be better for them to place their money where they cannot get it without much trouble and delay. But I have not much sympathy with this class of people, anyway. They do not amount to anything, and I am not in favor of establishing any method of investment for their benefit.

The savings bank deposit has another advantage over other forms of investment because the bank is willing to take small deposits, enabling one to begin with a dollar, and to deposit systematically. Each dollar draws the full rate of interest from the beginning of each quarter.

Let us suppose, for example, that you can save a dollar a week. You can deposit this dollar every week in a savings bank, while you cannot possibly invest it, dollar for dollar, in any other way. You may keep it in the bank until it reaches a thousand dollars or more, or until you have sufficient money to purchase a mortgage, a bond, or other security, or you can open an account in another bank, if your bank refuses to receive over a thousand dollars from any one depositor. If you are satisfied with four per cent, and you cannot get more than five per cent with much degree of safety, you may prefer to let your money remain in the bank, or to use several savings banks. Thousands of wealthy people, who know how to invest money, use savings banks exclusively or partially, depositing even as much as hundreds of thousands of dollars in them. They receive, usually, four per cent, and their money is secure, if they use good banks.

Some systematic savers and investors use savings banks as a legitimate make-shift. As fast as their accumulation reaches the proper size they withdraw it, that they may invest it in something paying a little higher interest, which may and may not be done at a risk.

I would recommend to every one that he use the savings bank at the start as the basic depository for his savings, whether or not he passes his money through the bank to something else. Further, I would advise all who begin to save, not only to use the savings bank, but to make their deposits systematically and conscientiously, and never to withdraw their funds for any other investment, unless they are sure that the security offered is as sound and as safe as the bank is, or nearly so.

Every one, unless he has accumulated considerable property, should make it a point to deposit something in the savings bank every week or every month.

This saving, and systematic depositing, should become a matter of principle. If the saver determines to save something at stated periods, he should make a deposit on each day decided upon, even though it be only a dollar. To break from this systematic saving rule interferes with the very principles of saving, economy, and protection.

Anything worth doing at all should be done systematically. Without system we do nothing well, and mighty little at all.

He who systematically saves, no matter how small the amount may be that he puts aside, has one good qualification, at least, and is doing something which every sensible business man respects and will accept as substantial proof of good character, faithfulness, stick-to-it-iveness, and ability.

Even a weekly or monthly visit to the savings bank makes for good, for the depositor comes face to face with men of standing, and often with men of mark, and their acquaintance or friendship is worth cultivating. The depositor, who periodically calls at the savings bank, gradually attracts the attention of the bank officials, and this acquaintance, although it may not be intimate, is likely to be of some use to him.

Many a business man gives decided preference, when engaging a clerk, to one who has a savings bank deposit.

A savings bank book of deposit is a positive

asset. It stands for more than its face value. It is a book of recommendation as well as of deposit.

I would advise every young person, and every one of any age, who has not begun to save, to make a savings bank deposit to-day. If he has only a dollar at his disposal, it is a start in the right direction, and the right start seldom ends at the wrong place.

Take care of your book of deposit. Do not leave it in a bureau drawer. If you have no safe deposit box, ask some friend of yours to take care of your book for you. If it is lost or stolen, immediately notify the bank by telephone, telegraph, or mail. It is quite difficult, however, for the wrong person to realize upon the book, but it is possible for him to obtain the money.

CHAPTER XIII

THE UNITED STATES GOVERNMENT BOND

THE United States Government bond represents what may be considered as absolute security. It is practically impossible for the holder of it to lose his money as long as our government remains intact and enjoys a fair degree of prosperity.

Theoretically speaking, the intrinsic value of the bond is not completely fixed, and it is possible for it to drop below its face value; but, practically, it remains firm and sound, its fluctuation being limited mostly to the premium paid by its purchaser.

The government can, of course, repudiate its indebtedness, but this is something which never has occurred, and there is not the slightest possibility of its occurrence.

Should the government fail, it is obvious that all forms of American securities would be valueless or close to worthless.

The United States Government bond is, and always will be, the standard investment, the one thing which may be considered superlatively safe.

The only objection to investing in these bonds is that they pay the lowest rate of interest upon their face value, the purchaser being seldom able to procure them without the payment of a premium. These bonds hardly ever reach the individual purchaser at par. They are usually bought by underwriters, who bid for the entire issue, and then job them out, so to speak, to individual purchasers, who must pay a premium to obtain them. This lowers the net receivable rate of interest.

There are two kinds of United States Government bonds,— registered and coupon.

The registered bond, as its name implies, is registered or recorded in the name of its purchaser or owner. If it is lost or destroyed the government will make good.

The coupon bond is payable to bearer or holder, and is practically the same as a bank-bill, except that interest is paid upon it. It is negotiable without registration. If it is lost it cannot be replaced. Owners of coupon bonds should make a memorandum of the numbers and place it in some secure place away from where the bonds are kept. A knowledge of these numbers may assist the owner in recovering them, if they should be lost or stolen. Coupon bonds should never be kept in an ordinary office or house safe, which may not give sufficient protection, but should be placed in a safe deposit box or other secure receptacle.

I would not particularly advise the wage-earner or salary-receiver to purchase United States Government bonds, or to consider them for investment purposes, and I say this knowing that these bonds offer the very maximum of security. The fact that they cannot be had except at a proportionately high premium, and that they pay the lowest rate of interest, is my reason for here advising against them, but be it understood that I would not take this stand if there were not other kinds of investment substantially as secure, although, theoretically, they may not be so, which pay a higher rate of interest.

The strong savings bank, for example, not only pays more interest, but is practically as safe as is the government itself, and the deposit in it is net, the interest being reckoned on what the depositor puts in. Further, there is no premium condition.

While I am thoroughly opposed to any form of investment, for the wage-earner and salary-receiver, which presents more than the minimum of risk, I see no reason why he should content himself with so low a rate of interest as is paid by the government bond, when practically the same security is obtainable with higher interest.

The province of the government bond seems to be principally for large investors, to those in charge of trust estates of considerable size, and to those who desire to salt-down, so to speak, large sums of money, which may remain unmolested and free from attention and care.

I would advise the small investor to get all he can for his money, provided he does not take undue risk. He may obtain a fair rate of interest, with substantial security, by depositing his money in a strong savings bank, or by using other conservative methods, which I have spoken of in this book, and which pay from three and one-half to five per cent.

Let me say here, as I have said several times in this book, that the minimum of risk accompanies only investments paying not more than five per cent, with an occasional opportunity of six per cent. The line of safety may be drawn at five per cent, although there are a few investments paying six per cent, which are reasonably safe.

For the foregoing reasons only do I refuse to recommend in particular government bonds to those who can save but a little money.

However, if one desires to possess the feeling which comes from *absolute* security, and wants to have his money where he need never give it a second thought, willing that it should earn the lowest rate of interest, he would make no mistake in purchasing government bonds, preferably registered bonds, and placing them in a safe deposit box, where robbery and loss appear to be impossible.

The owner of the registered government bond cannot possibly lose his property. The owner of the coupon government bond is subject only to the possibility of his safe deposit box being broken into,— something which has never occurred so far as I know.

But as there are so many other forms of investment practically as strong, although theoretically weaker, and which pay a higher rate of interest, the small investor can get along without holding United States Government bonds.

CHAPTER XIV

THE STATE, MUNICIPAL, AND TOWN BOND

PERHAPS there is in America a State, city, or town free from indebtedness. If there is, I have never heard of it, and I do not know of any one who has.

Money is borrowed by States, municipalities, and towns for various purposes and according to law, usually in anticipation of taxes and to pay current expenses, and for the establishment of public improvements, like water-works and sewers.

Comparatively few communities could enjoy any of the modern improvements or betterments, if the money for their construction was not borrowed, either on notes signed by the proper officials, or by the issue of bonds. Very few improvements are made without the issuing of bonds, for most of the money obtained on notes is for current expenses.

The borrowing capacity of any State, municipality, or town is limited by law; but the State may legally, at its discretion, move the borrowing line ahead, even near to the danger point, and occasionally it allows it to be passed.

The State borrows money through act of its

legislature or assembly, the municipality by vote of its city government, and the town by vote of the town itself, subject in all cases to State law or regulation.

When borrowing is done within the prescribed limits of indebtedness, without special State concession, and by legal act of the officials or voters, the bonds issued are what may be considered close to absolute security, and are to be recommended to the small investor, and to others who would prefer a fair rate of interest with solid security.

These bonds pay a low rate of interest, never exceeding five per cent, and frequently as low as four or three and one-half per cent, except where the borrowing community is heavily in debt, which condition raises the element of risk.

For example, the conservative, economically managed city, with less than normal indebtedness, can borrow money at a low rate of interest, even at three and one-half or four per cent, and yet sell its bonds above par, individuals or banking houses buying the entire issue at a premium of from one to even eight per cent.

Let us suppose that a conservative city desires to construct new water-works. The city's indebtedness is below the limit prescribed by law, its credit is good, it is progressive and growing, the security it offers is ample, and there is a certainty that both interest and principal will be promptly paid.

Unless money is especially tight, it can borrow at from three and one-half to four per cent; literally for less, because it can dispose of its bonds at a premium, a thousand-dollar bond selling for from one thousand and ten dollars to occasionally as much as one thousand and eighty dollars. These bonds are usually sold to brokers, bankers, and underwriters, who sell them to the public at a slight increase. If the broker pays, say, one thousand and thirty dollars for a thousand-dollar bond, he would probably sell this bond at from one thousand and thirty-five to one thousand and forty dollars, or for more.

As a rule it is difficult to obtain a bond direct from the town or city, unless you are a capitalist or a member of a syndicate.

It is obvious that a four per cent bond, sold at a premium, does not pay four per cent net to its purchaser, who may not receive more than three and one-half to three and seven-eighths per cent on the purchase price.

The intrinsic value of the bond is also dependent upon the length of time it runs, the thirty- or forty-year bond being worth more than the ten-year bond.

If the State, city, or town borrowing is in a

good financial condition, and its bonds are legally and properly issued, they may be considered as offering a security practically as sound as that presented by the United States Government bond.

The bonds of communities of fair credit are reasonably safe, but those carrying large indebtedness, which must borrow by special permit of the State, should be avoided by the small and careful investor.

Upon general principles I would advise the small investor to have nothing to do with a bond paying over four per cent, unless a half dozen good financiers, who are not interested in the bonds in question, expressed emphatically the most favorable opinion concerning them; but under no circumstances would I advise the purchase of a bond paying over five per cent, unless one is able to take speculative chances.

Bear in mind that a bond cannot possibly pay more than the rate of interest specified upon its face. If it is a four per cent bond, for example, it can never give its owner more than four per cent, while a share of stock may pay any dividend; but the security offered by the average stock is far below that given by the average bond.

There are some disadvantages to investing in bonds:

First, because of the low rate of interest paid;

but this condition prevails with all safe investments and should not be considered an objection.

Secondly, because the selling value of bonds may fluctuate. They may be worth more to-day than to-morrow; but when this occurs, the fluctuations are likely to be small, although I have known a high grade of city bond to drop six or seven points in a year, not from the face value of the bond, but from the premium paid on it. For example, let us suppose that you pay one thousand and sixty dollars for a thousand-dollar bond, It is possible that within a year or more you cannot sell this bond in the open market for more than a thousand and ten or a thousand and twenty dollars. If you are forced to sell, your loss is considerable. There is, however, a fair chance that the premium will return to what you paid, or close to that figure. You sustain no loss, then, or only a slight loss, if you can afford to hold the bond. I would advise you, however, not to purchase bonds at a high premium. Better wait until the condition of the money market is such that safe bonds are selling nearer to par. Your banker, or other financial adviser, will tell you what to do, not only what to purchase, but when to purchase. Better keep your money in the savings bank until the bond market is low.

Thirdly, the danger of losing a bond unless it

is registered; but a box in a good safe deposit vault gives absolute security. The registered bonds are safer, of course, but many prefer the unregistered ones, because they are more negotiable and can be sold with no formality.

The fluctuation of first-class bonds is invariably due to the condition of the money market, and their holders are not likely to lose on them, if they purchased them at a fair premium and can afford to hold them over a slump in the market.

The advantages of a good bond are:

First, it is considered by all first-class financiers, high-grade bankers, and conservative investors as offering pretty close to absolute security. A high-grade bond is a legal investment for all savings banks and is looked upon as the best form of security for a loan.

Secondly, its easy negotiability. A good bond is seldom worth less than its face value and is about as good as a bank bill. Any bank will gladly loan from eighty to ninety per cent of its face value, holding the bond as security. As a matter of fact, the owner of a bond has what is substantially a negotiable bank bill, yet paying a fair rate of interest.

There are on the market large quantities of fraudulent, illegal, and worthless bonds, issued by mushroom towns, and other communities, which are heavily in debt and without credit. These bonds are offered by irresponsible brokers, and usually promise to pay a high rate of interest. They are generally handsomely printed upon a high grade of paper, and the face of them presents an impressive appearance. Occasionally these bad bonds are guaranteed to pay but a low rate of interest, this being done to avert suspicion.

Because some bonds offer the very maximum of security, many people look upon all bonds as safe. This common belief enables dishonest brokers to dispose of worthless bonds. As a rule, do not purchase bonds issued at distant places, because it may not be easy for you to ascertain their value, and somewhat difficult to obtain expert opinion regarding them.

The majority of banking houses and brokers dealing in bonds are thoroughly reliable, still I would not advise the small investor to place implicit confidence in any one party, especially in any one seller of bonds. He should investigate for himself. It is easy to look up the financial standing of a town. He may make inquiries of the presidents and cashiers of two or three good banks, who would gladly impart the information desired. The value of good bonds is known to all bankers and men of finance, residing in the community, especially to the bankers, for bonds are a convenient and satisfactory form of collateral at the banks.

To make myself plain, let me suppose, for example, that you think seriously of purchasing a certain municipal bond. Before doing so, I would advise you to call upon two or more first-class bankers, and ask their opinion regarding the security offered. If you are advised strongly by all of them to purchase the bonds, you can safely do so. If the opinion is not unanimous, let them alone.

Bonds which pay exceeding four per cent do not present the best security, although a few four and one-half and five per cent bonds are reasonably safe. The community paying more than four per cent for money is usually financially weak or is very much in debt.

Comparatively few high-grade bonds are more than modestly advertised. Some are never advertised at all. Upon general principles, I would advise you to have nothing to do with a bond which is heavily advertised. A good bond does not need much publicity.

Remember that this book is not intended for speculators, or for financial gamblers, men who play with stocks and bonds as they do with cards, to win or lose at the casting of the dice. I am presenting facts and opinions, which I hope will be of service to the rank and file of men and women of the great middle class, to the many thousands who have small incomes, and cannot save, therefore, more than moderate sums, and who should consider security of more consequence than a high rate of interest.

I do not propose to compare the good bond with the savings bank, because the first-class savings bank offers as substantial security as the bond does, although the high-grade or gilt-edged bond is safer than the average savings bank account. Both the good bond and the thoroughly secure savings bank pay about the same rate of interest, and offer practically the same security. It is largely a question of preference. I would advise the small investor to use both.

CHAPTER XV

BANK STOCK

NATIONAL bank stocks or shares are considered high-class securities, their value being based upon the capital of the bank itself, the quality and quantity of the business done, and, further, upon the reliability and financial standing of the directors and officers.

National banks fail, but not often; and comparatively few which are officered by men of money and high standing meet with more than temporary embarrassment.

The stock of the conservative, and yet progressive and well managed national bank, may be considered as giving pretty close to the maximum of safety. Yet it is subject to some fluctuations, and the holder of it cannot depend upon its value remaining at any one price. But these fluctuations are usually quite small, the stock remaining, as a rule, at its standard valuation. If it drops, the decline is likely to be momentary, with a quick return to the normal.

The purchaser of national bank shares should bear in mind that he is personally liable for twice the amount of his stock, should the bank suffer financial embarrassment and not be able to meet its obligations. For example, let us suppose that you own one share of national bank stock, the par value of which is one hundred dollars. The bank fails, and there is not sufficient money to pay its depositors. A depositor is a preferred creditor, and he must be paid before any one else receives his money. Therefore, you, as a stockholder, may be assessed as much as the par value of your stock, in which case your loss would be one hundred dollars plus what you paid for the stock.

Many a small investor has been ruined because of the failure of the national bank in which he is a stockholder.

This condition adds additional risk to national bank stock, yet it is comparatively small as a matter of fact, because most national banks are strong financially.

Before purchasing national bank stock it is well to investigate the standing of the bank, and to ascertain the market or selling value of the shares for the last ten to twenty years. If the stock has shown much fluctuation, better let it alone. Then, you should consult, personally or by mail, the officers of other banks and men of high financial reputation, who are in a position to know about the bank in question, or can easily ascertain for you various facts relative to its standing.

Unless several reliable bank officials, or other recognized financiers, will unqualifiedly recommend the stock, you had better consider some other form of investment.

The national bank is a public institution. If it is solid, and doing a good business, its position in the financial world is well known, and you will have little difficulty in getting at the facts.

If, on the other hand, you experience difficulty in finding out about it, the chances are that there is something wrong about the bank.

Comparatively few national bank stocks sell at par, and the premium may run to many times the face value of the stock, the size of the premium depending upon the reliability of the bank, its capitalization, and the interest paid.

The share-holder is not likely to receive more than five or six per cent for his investment, even though the bank may pay double or treble that sum on the par value of its stock.

The stock of a first-class national bank never sells at par, and there are instances where it is worth thirty times its face value.

Never buy a bank stock selling for less than par. It may be safe, but not for you.

As a matter of fact, good national bank stock

is not likely to be a much better paying investment than is a deposit in a good savings bank or a good municipal bond.

While I have every respect for good national bank stock, I do not especially recommend it to wage-earners, because it is preëminently an investment for men of money, is somewhat subject to fluctuation, carries with it a liability, and does not pay much more interest than that given by savings banks, where the deposit is not subject to fluctuation, and where the depositor has no responsibility. The security offered, however, by a good national bank, is very much above that given to the depositors of many savings banks, which are virtually controlled by one man, and which are too small to stand defalcation or loss.

When I refer to good savings banks, I have in mind only those controlled by several men of high standing, and carrying so much money that it would be extremely difficult for them to be affected by dishonesty or other disaster.

I need not discuss the stock of the state bank and loan and trust company. What I have said about national bank stock applies virtually to that of other banking institutions.

The reader is referred to the chapter entitled "Keeping a Bank Account" for further information about business banks.

CHAPTER XVI

THE INVESTMENT VALUE OF STOCKS

I HAVE attempted to cover in other chapters the various kinds of stocks, and I have dealt particularly upon the speculative side of stock buying. In this chapter I shall try to treat, briefly, stocks as an investment for the man of small income, the salary-receiver, and the wage-earner, without any attempt to consider them for the speculator and capitalist.

It is obvious that the man of little present money, and with small prospect of accumulating more than a moderate sum, should consider safety and security of far more importance than the large profit which may be realized by the taking of more than ordinary chances and by speculation.

A share of stock may be untechnically described as a piece of paper representing a proportionate part of the ownership of a corporation; for example, if a company is incorporated for one hundred thousand dollars, and issues one thousand shares at one hundred dollars each, the holder of one share owns one one-thousandth part of the corporation and the property held by the corporation. The holding of this share entitles its owner to one vote; if he holds two shares, he has two votes.

The real or permanent value, but, unfortunately, not always the selling price, of stock is dependent wholly upon the assets of the corporation and its present or prospective profits. Practically all corporations are controlled by one man, or by a few men, and the small stockholder has little or no voice in the management. The majority of stock controls, and a majority vote of the stock itself, not of the stockholders, elects the directors, frames the policy of action, and virtually handles the situation.

Let us suppose, for example, that there are forty stockholders, holding one thousand shares altogether, but that one man holds five hundred and one of the shares; he is practically manager of the company, and may do as he pleases with it, provided he does not permit provable irregularities under the law.

The minority stockholders have rights, but it is exceedingly difficult for them to exercise them. The stockholders in control may do as they please to an almost unlimited extent.

As a matter of fact, comparatively few corporations are other than partnerships, the stockholders, except those holding a majority of the stock, are less in control than silent partners are, and usually have less power and fewer rights. Large enterprises, and even small ones, are incorporated, because by so doing, the owners escape, as a rule, personal liability and responsibility; and because it is easier to sell stock, and thereby obtain outside capital, than it is to raise money under a partnership.

Practically all corporation stock is subject to fluctuation, although the best stocks seldom move more than a few points up or down. Stock may pay any rate of interest, or none at all, and it may be purchased for ten cents on a dollar, or less, or for many times its face value. If it pays a dividend exceeding six per cent, and the corporation is well managed and has large assets, it is not likely to sell at par, and it may be worth twenty or thirty times more than its par value, although comparatively few stocks sell for more than double their face value. A stock paying, say, twelve per cent, may sell in the market for twice its par value. This would mean that its purchaser would realize but six per cent. No share of solid, legitimate stock, paying a good rate of interest, is likely to be obtainable at a price which would allow a net dividend exceeding six or seven per cent.

As the share of stock represents ownership and

management, and is not a mortgage lien upon the property, it does not have the intrinsic value of a bond; nor does it give the same security. It pays a larger rate of interest, because its value is more speculative, and its owner takes a larger risk than does the holder of a bond.

Preferred stock may be described as that holding a preference over common stock. Should the corporation fail or liquidate, the bond-holders, and those having mortgage or other liens upon the property, are paid first. Then come the preferred stockholders, then the owners of the common stock. Preferred stock may and may not have a higher intrinsic value than that of common stock, and it may sell for less. If the common stock is paying a large dividend, it will bring very much more than preferred stock will, but if the company is suffering from disaster or financial weakness preferred stock offers greater security.

The interest on the preferred stock cannot be over the amount specified upon its face, even though the common stock may be paying ten times as large a dividend. If the company is not doing a good business, it cannot pay, of course, the full rate of interest guaranteed to the preferred stockholders. They are not sure of receiving the interest agreed upon, but they are sure of not receiving more than the interest agreed upon.

The full amount of interest specified on the preferred stock must be paid before the common stockholders receive any dividend.

Would I advise the man with a small income to consider either preferred or common stock as an investment? I do not feel justified in answering by an enthusiastic "yes," or by an emphatic "no."

Stock buying, selling, and holding belong rightly to men of money, to professional financiers, and to those who can afford to take more or less speculative chances. It is obvious that the average salary-receiver, and that all wage-earners, are not in a position to take more than the very minimum of risk, nor can they afford to invest their money, as a rule, in anything which is likely to fluctuate in value. I would not advise them, necessarily, against holding a few shares of gilt-edged stock, of standard stock, of stock which is more likely to go up than to go down, of stock which cannot under other than extraordinary conditions drop more than a few points. Such stock exists, but it cannot often be purchased so as to pay exceeding six per cent.

Unless one is thoroughly familiar with the stock market, or has conservative friends who are investors rather than speculators, to whom he can go for advice, he had better let stocks severely alone, partly because the security offered is not likely to be as good as that presented by the strong savings bank and the solid bond; and, further, because when one begins to buy stocks he is likely to become infatuated with what may be called a sport, and this tendency, which frequently becomes chronic, usually results in disaster.

The reader is requested to study the other chapters on stocks, especially the one entitled "Speculating in Stocks."

CHAPTER XVII

SPECULATING IN STOCKS

WHILE the element of luck, or chance, or speculation, accompanies all business-doing, and cannot avoid being a component part of every investment, and of everything which represents value, the so-called stock speculator operates along lines diametrically opposite to those usually employed by the ordinary business man, and to those necessary to the conduct of regular business, like the manufacturing and selling of commodities.

The action of business, and the principle of conducting it, are either based, or supposed to be based, upon the making and distributing of intrinsic values, things which may be measured or weighed.

Stocks may have, or should have, a definite value; yet many of them are purely speculative, selling high to-day and low to-morrow, and the owner of them may, at no time, have more than a small equity in what he owns or thinks he owns.

The commodity or general merchandise may be subject to the fluctuations of the market, but its value usually remains the same, or about the same, except under unusual conditions.

The stock may and may not have intrinsic value. Its selling price is often problematic. It is likely to sell for more than it is worth to-day, and less than it is worth to-morrow; and, if it is worth nothing, it is by no means impossible to sell it for something, if it is held by those who know how to manipulate it; but the small investor is never in that class.

If the corporation has a negotiable asset equal to its stock issue, and this asset is likely to remain permanent, then each share of stock has a definite value, subject to minor fluctuations; but if the stock represents "water," and has only an inflated value, or is part real and part "water," then it can have no standard price and little basis of actual valuation. Even the best of stocks are subject to fluctuations, caused, not necessarily by a shrinkage in the actual valuation, or because of increased or decreased business, but because a syndicate of underwriters and manipulators are playing a game with them, with the public on the other side; and in this contest, the public seldom wins. For example, a railroad has certain negotiable assets, consisting of its right-of-way, its rolling-stock, its real estate, and the business it is doing. Its stock, therefore, unless there be a flood of business or a general depression in business, should be worth the same to-day as it was yesterday, and yet it may go up or down a few points in twenty-four hours. If it goes down, the owner of it loses money, unless it soon goes up again or he can afford to carry it. The regular commodities and merchandise are influenced also by financial movements, but are not as sensitive as stocks are, and are subject to less fluctuation.

The trading in stocks which represent intrinsic values is a thoroughly legitimate business, and there is no business reason why it should not be carried on by men who understand it.

The stock market is preëminently the exclusive arena for those who enjoy fighting, and who know how to fight, who laugh at success and who smile at failure; but it is not for the outsider, and the so-called tenderfoot. It is easier for him to walk on the red hot pricks of trade than it is for him to travel through the mazes of the stock market.

Stock buying and selling is a business in itself. Success depends upon a thorough knowledge of the situation, but even the closest familiarity with the business may avail for nought in the long run. A large proportion of stock manipulators, and dealers in stocks, even of the better class, may be completely swamped by the rise and fall of the market. They were rich yesterday, and are poor to-day.

The great highway of life is lined on both sides with former inmates of the stock exchange, men who once travelled by automobile, and are now either dead or are crawling into obscurity.

The stock market, from the curb to the legitimate exchange, is the cause of more failures than can be laid against any dozen other business factors put together.

The majority of small investors keep away, or are kept away, from standard stocks. They inhabit bucket-shops, and surround the offices of low-class brokers, who sell less-than-nothing, nothing, or almost nothing, for something. The very atmosphere of the bucket-shop, like that of the gambling-den, attracts them and holds them. They are intoxicated with greed. They care nothing for honor, or for anything else in their mad rush to get rich mighty quick. They are gamblers, neither more nor less.

The bucket-shop is, generally defined, a brokerage institution, where all kinds of stocks,— good, bad, and worse, usually the last,— are sold on illegitimate margin, the purchaser seldom having any tangible equity, and often no ownership in what he thinks he has purchased.

The bucket-shop proprietor plays to win, plays his customer to lose, and he always plays with loaded stocks as he would play with loaded dice. Occasionally the customer is permitted to win, that the bucket-shop proprietor may fleece him in the end.

Bucket-shops are usually handsomely furnished and made extremely attractive to their customers, who are offered every superficial courtesy, even to free letter-paper, telephone, and postage stamps.

Hundreds of thousands of men, and thousands of women, owe their downfall to speculation in stocks, and most of them have reached the pit of despair through the open way of the bucket-shop. They know nothing about stock values, and they buy them as they would match pennies, virtually staking their money upon the turn of the fraudulent wheel of fortune. If they win, luck or accident is responsible for it. If they lose, they receive their deserts. Where one small investor wins at stock gambling, or at stock buying, a hundred lose, and practically all of them go down in the end.

The mania for stock gambling (I put it this way instead of calling it speculation) is as fatal as is that which makes a man a slave to liquor or opium. It gets a grip upon him to his certain ruination. It becomes a chronic disease. It is infectious and epidemic.

No one can afford to dabble in stocks in a

speculative way, either through the bucket-shops or the regular exchange, or to buy high-grade stocks or those of questionable value, unless he is financially able to stand many and frequent losses, and has the mental capacity to look disaster in the face without flinching; and, further, is so situated that his downfall will not affect others who are innocent. He must take chances such as a man of moderate means has no moral or other right to take.

Stock speculation for the man of small income, or for the rich man of inexperience, is as far removed from the legitimate and careful investment as the cold of the North is distant from the heat of the Equator.

I have heard that there are, located in some mysterious somewhere, a few small investors who have successfully played the game of speculation, who have won by luck, and yet had sense enough to pocket their profits and stop at the right time; but I am bound to say that I have never been permitted to rest my eyes upon one of these speculative wonders, and I never have been face to face with any one who has seen any one of them or could give me his address.

There is an immutable law which makes it well-nigh impossible for the gambler either to save, or to continuously win, or to come out more than whole, at best. But even if he could break even, and make a fair profit, I would protest against any form of stock gambling, or any kind of stock speculation, for the man of small income:

First, because it is morally wrong for him, anyway, whether or not it be right for the man of money.

Secondly, because every form of gambling, including speculation, leads to financial degradation and is responsible for a large part of our business dishonor, and for premature failure and disaster.

Thirdly, because no man of little money, with a family dependent upon him, or even one without dependents, can afford to take speculative chances. To do so discounts his present and mortgages his future.

I have never known a speculator, even one of pronounced success, to recommend speculation, certainly not to the salary-receiver and wage-earner. He would no more think of giving this advice than would the opium fiend advocate the opium habit.

To take more than fair chances, to enter into speculation, if one has only a moderate income and has a family, is as criminally wrong as it is to rob the cash-drawer.

I am speaking emphatically, because I realize

the danger, and because I know what I am talking about.

I would advise the small investor, the man of family, unless he be wealthy, the salary-receiver, the wage-earner, and the average man, to shun the stock market, and particularly the bucket-shop side of it, as he would the plague. I would even go so far as to advise him never to invest his money in fluctuating stocks, even if he is reasonably sure of winning, because the glory of the initial victory may lead him on to financial disaster.

Many a small investor goes into stock buying because he has received that peculiar something, or that indescribable nothing, which is know as a "tip." Ninety-nine and nine-tenths of the so-called "tips" are intentionally misleading. People who have "tips" good for anything, usually have brains enough to keep them to themselves. Most of the "tips" have strings tied to them, and hooks inside of them. They are usually baits cast, not by fishers of fish, not by fishers of men, but plain, every-day catchers of that peculiar wiggling and irresponsible form of life known on the street under the very appropriate and significant title of "suckers."

When you have a little money, and do not know

what to do with it, do not speculate with it. Better stick to the old-fashioned stocking, which has but one hole, and that an entrance, or to the pantry sugar bowl, which does not spill its contents if it is kept right side up.

CHAPTER XVIII

BUYING STOCKS ON MARGIN

STOCKS are purchased by payments in full, or by substantial partial payments, or they are bought, or apparently so, on what is commercially known as " margin."

While a " margin " is virtually a partial payment, it is appropriately called a " margin," because of its smallness.

A first-class or reputable broker is not supposed to sell on " margin," except under special conditions, and even then he is not likely to receive less than a very substantial payment on account. An unreliable, disreputable, and usually thoroughly dishonest, broker or dealer in stocks almost invariably sells on small " margin," and in comparatively few of his transactions is there a payment in full, or a payment anywhere near to the selling price of the stock.

The usual " margin " is as low as is conducive to the broker's, not the investor's, safety, the former requiring a payment just large enough to cover any probable depression in the market or selling price of the stock.

The bucket-shop proprietor and margin-man

invariably deal to win, and never use their own money in the play. Their customers are usually small investors,— the "lambs" in the street,— who possess neither financial knowledge, nor much of any other kind, victims of acute avarice, foolish moths who fly about the speculative lamp, occasionally, and usually by accident, keeping out of the flame, but always getting burned in the end.

The usual "margin" required by the broker is about ten per cent of the real or imaginary market value of the stock. For example, if the probable selling price of the stock is ten dollars per share, the broker demands a deposit of one dollar, for which he will purchase the stock or pretend to do so, and either carry it or claim to carry it for his customer. If the stock goes up, say, to twelve dollars, the broker will, or will say that he will, upon the customer's request, sell the stock and give the customer three dollars, less his commission; but in ninety-nine cases out of a hundred, the broker will so play upon the lack of judgment of his customer that the customer will reinvest his profits on "margin." If the stock goes down, say, to eight dollars, then the customer has lost the dollar which he deposited, and must pay the broker another dollar, or lose his stock.

Most of the stock supposed to have been

purchased on "margin" is never really bought at all. The broker carries the transaction on paper. If the customer loses, he demands further payment. If the customer wins, he does his best to keep him from taking his profits, and suggests reinvesting, and so on to the end of the customer.

Margin-buyers are virtually gamblers on paper, and their profits may remain on paper, but their losses are real.

Theoretically it would appear that the purchase of stocks on "margin" is not inconsistent with good business principles. If it is, then it might be claimed consistently that the buying of real estate upon mortgage, or incurring any kind of indebtedness, should be discouraged, and that we should fall back upon the old-fashioned notion that no one has a right to anything which he cannot fully pay for in cash or its equivalent. But fortunately or unfortunately, getting into debt has become, by custom, a legitimate part of business-doing.

Comparatively few business men, whether speculators or not, pay in full for what they receive when they receive it. Some of them believe that running an account or getting trusted is better business policy than to make full payments invariably in cash. Let us suppose, for example, that a man can purchase goods, either on long credit or by a payment of from twenty-five to fifty per cent of the face of the bill, and that a full cash payment would not save him more than two per cent. This is considered good business, provided the man has solid assets, and can, if he will, meet the indebtedness, and, further, provided that the use of ready money is worth more to him than the discount he would receive for cash.

Getting into debt is, therefore, perfectly legitimate, or has been made so by custom. If it is not overused, it is not to be condemned generally, for most of the harm in it is due to the degree of it and not to the action itself.

Indebtedness may be both a business virtue and a business curse.

The right proportion of indebtedness is not dishonest, but too much of it is positively dangerous, runs clear up to the line of failure, and is often the basis of criminal dishonesty.

Do not misunderstand me, and do not think that I am encouraging debt of any kind, except where it pays to get into debt. No one has a right to purchase anything which he is not reasonably sure of being able to pay for. If he runs into debt he should have business reasons for so doing,— reasons of expediency, not of probable inability to make good. To incur any other than a safe indebtedness is not only dishonest, but works injury to the doer, perhaps not at first, but his downfall is certain in the end.

Common business indebtedness,— the raising of money upon mortgage or other security,— is in principle and in fact diametrically different from buying stock on "margin." It is difficult to explain this, for theoretically they are alike, but practically they are far removed from each other, particularly in result.

Comparatively few careful borrowers meet with disaster on account of the transaction, while practically every buyer of stock on "margin" is either a heavy loser or finds himself wiped off of the financial slate. In this particular case, may we not judge the action by the result, and not attempt to analyse too minutely the component parts of the transaction itself.

Most emphatically I would advise the small investor to refuse absolutely to purchase stocks of any kind on any size of "margin," even on safe "margin." It is better for him, as a matter of principle and for safety, to make full payment for the stock he buys, or not to buy it at all. True, a "margin" may be safe to the man who understands the market, assuming that any one really knows it, but the "margin" practice is decidedly risky and is the cause of most of the financial downfalls of small speculators.

The bucket-shop or margin-broker is dishonest because he is breaking both a written and an unwritten but firmly established financial law. If he is dishonest he cannot be trusted, and if he cannot be trusted, he should not be patronized.

It is never safe to deal with a swindler, whether you are buying stocks or horses. Even if you know stocks and horses, he will get the better of you sooner or later, unless you are a swindler yourself, and then you will take turns with him, each alternately getting the better of the other.

The stock gambler and small investor patronize the bucket-shop or margin-shop because there the dollar appears to go further than it would with a legitimate broker. The bucket-shop or margin-man cares nothing for the customer, in fact his customer's loss is likely to be his gain. He would not be successful if his customer's interest received any real attention other than the encouragement which draws the customer deeper into the mire. He encourages the sale of stocks on "margin," and will take the smallest "margin" consistent with safety to himself.

Many of these so-called brokers never purchase any stock, except when forced to make good, and it often requires threats of arrest to compel them to meet their obligations. Their dealings are often wholly on paper, and the customer has, at best, mere gambling chances.

The customer is always at a disadvantage, for the broker invariably deals to win, and he wins anyway, whether or not his customer loses.

Buying stocks on " margin " is not only pure and simple gambling, but it is more dishonest than gambling, because the gambler's pot may contain some tangible property, while the margin-gambler usually plays upon paper, with small actual chance of collecting his winnings, if he should appear to win, and with the absolute certainty of being obliged to pay his losses.

More men have been ruined by buying stocks on " margin " than in any other direction, and the practice is to be condemned without even a suggestion of qualification. Where one margin-dealer makes a dollar, thousands lose ten dollars, and all of them eventually go to pieces. The stock gambler, and particularly he who purchases stocks on " margin," takes more desperate chances than does the buyer of lottery tickets or the better on horse races. The lottery ticket usually represents an opportunity, although a very small one, of getting something, and some of the horse-race gamblers have to win; but statistics show conclusively that the small investor is absolutely sure of losing in the end if he buys stocks on "margin" or attempts to get rich by speculating in stocks.

In many States bucket-shops are prohibited by law, but one may gamble in stocks, if he will, without the aid of the bucket-shop, and without buying stocks on "margin." The small investor or man of low income has no business to dabble in stocks, whether he buys them outright or on "margin," unless he is willing to take unfair chances, and to assume the very maximum of risk, and is foolish enough to be willing to stake his all on the prospect of doubling his money.

He may possibly make money for a time by speculating in stocks. Even if he takes ninety-nine chances out of one hundred he may occasionally win, and sometimes luck seems to be with him, and he is able to trump every transaction; but experience shows, beyond a doubt, that the small investor invariably loses sooner or later, usually sooner. True, he should have sense enough to stop after he has made some success, but he does not stop; for the man of small income, who is foolish enough to speculate, has usually not brains enough to be satisfied with any moderate degree of profit, and is pretty sure to remain in the game until everything he has staked is gone.

Unless he understands the stock market, the farther he keeps away from it, the better off he is.

The bucket- or margin-shop is one of the most largely patronized gates to financial hell.

CHAPTER XIX

INDUSTRIAL STOCK

INDUSTRIAL stock is a share in the property, good-will, and profits of a private corporation doing business under a charter issued to it by the State, without interference from any national or state law other than that which applies to corporations in general. It does not hold or operate under a franchise, has no *eminent domain* rights, and cannot use any property, unless it owns or leases it.

The private corporation is, in fact, a partnership for the doing of business, except that the ownership is vested in the share-holders, or stockholders.

During the last few years the incorporation of private business enterprises has become almost epidemic. Many a corner grocery store, and drug shop, are incorporated, although they may be doing a very moderate business. Formerly there were comparatively few private corporations other than those representing vast interests. Then, practically all business was done under copartnership.

The practical difference between a corporation

and a co-partnership is largely that the liability of the owners is limited in the former and less limited in the latter. Under common law, all co-partners are liable for each other's acts, and this liability may extend to personal property; while in a corporation, the stockholders or owners have no liability beyond their stock and the corporation property itself, except, sometimes, they may be held for a result of negligence. The ownership of a corporation is easily transferable, in whole or in part, much more so than it is in a co-partnership.

Industrial stock, then, simply represents a share in the ownership of a corporation doing business similar to that done under co-partnership, and is not a public service company, like those owning or controlling railroads, trolleys, gas, water, and electric light. For example, a firm of shoemakers desires to incorporate its business instead of continuing under a co-partnership. The company capitalizes at one hundred thousand dollars, issuing one thousand shares of stock at a par value of one hundred dollars each. In all probability one man, or a few men, will retain as many as five hundred and one shares, and will control the business, the minority of the stockholders having comparatively few rights against the majority, unless it transgresses the law. Four hundred and ninety-nine, or a less number, of shares of stock are offered for sale, or a part of them may be held in the treasury, to be sold later on, if it seems advisable to part with it. The stock of the company, other than the treasury stock, belongs to the individual holder of it, and not to the company, and he may or may not turn the receipts of its sale into the business, but the money coming from the sale of treasury stock cannot rightly be used for other than for the conduct or development of the business. But as the management is likely to be wholly in the hands of the majority of the stockholders, it is not at all difficult for the receipts coming from the treasury stock eventually to reach the pockets of the majority stockholders, and be of little benefit to the business, provided, of course, that the company is controlled by dishonest men and speculators.

Many private corporations issue what is known as preferred stock, as well as common stock. The preferred stock carries with it a real or apparent guarantee to pay a specified dividend, and is not allowed to pay any more, even if the business yields an enormous profit. Occasionally the company earns as high as thirty to fifty per cent, or even more, on its common stock, yet does not pay more than six to ten per cent on its preferred stock. (See description of preferred stock in the chapter entitled "The Investment Value of Stocks.")

During the last few years enormous quantities of industrial stock have been presented, and at times, fairly dumped upon the unsuspecting public. The newspapers have been filled with pages of advertising, most of which is printed in the brightest colors, over-burdened with sense-jarring adjectives, offering unparalleled and unprecedented opportunities of getting-rich-mighty-quick at hardly the suggestion of the minimum of cost.

The foregoing statements, though true, must not be construed to mean that all industrial stocks are other than sound and do not represent tangible property and probable dividends. The very nature of the law permitting the incorporation of private enterprises offers unusual opportunity for fraud, and gives, I believe, the largest market place for the successful sale of worthless, or next to worthless, stock. It enables men to swindle each other legally, and offers a premium on fraud and misrepresentation. Undoubtedly, it can be regulated, but not wholly controlled, by law. So long as lambs are born, there will be wolves to feed upon them.

The practical advantage of an industrial stock

as an investment, is that it is likely to pay a larger dividend than can possibly come from a sound and safe bond or other equally solid security. Some industrial stocks pay as much as ten per cent, and even fifty to one hundred per cent is not impossible, although comparatively few safe industrial stocks are likely to bring more than six to eight per cent, at the outside, except during "spurt years."

It is obvious that few good industrial stocks, heavily secured with property, would be sold at par, if they are paying more than a good rate of interest.

The average industrial stock does not pay an even dividend. It is likely to be high one year and low the next. It is subject to tremendous fluctuations, but the best industrial stock seldom pays less than six or seven per cent net on its selling price.

The disadvantages of industrial stock as an investment are:

First, it is likely to be subject to great fluctuation. The business may show large profits one year, and a loss the next.

Secondly, a change of management in the business may occur at any time. Bad management may lower the profits or break the business.

Thirdly, all private corporations, barring a

few illegal trusts, are subject to competition, and this competition may cripple or ruin the company.

Fourthly, comparatively few industrial companics own properties equal in intrinsic value to the amount of the stock issued, although in some cases the properties cost as much or more.

Fifthly, even well-equipped and modern factories will seldom bring what they cost when sold under the hammer. A broken business cannot often be mended to its original condition.

Sixthly, industrial corporations are usually controlled by one man, or a few men, and the death or disability of these men, or any dishonest practice on their part, is likely either to break the company or to materially affect the value of its stock.

Scattered over the country are hundreds of thousands of manufacturing and other concerns, which are loading their stock upon the public, giving the buyers practically no security, and very little prospect of receiving any dividends, save the first one, which may be paid for bait. Many of these corporations are officered by speculators, who manipulate them to their own advantage and to the customer's loss. They control the majority of the stock, although most of the money has come from the minority stockholders. Of course, minority stockholders have rights, but it is extremely difficult to get them, as the owners of the majority of the stock are usually able to override any protest from the minority.

I would not advise men of small means, or with moderate incomes, to give the preference to investment in industrial stocks. As a rule, I would most emphatically warn them against purchasing the stock of any industrial company which does not stand high in trade, which is not conservatively managed, and which is not recommended by high-class business men and bankers. Unless the stock will be considered as collateral by first-class banking houses, the small investor had better have nothing to do with it.

When one is an employee of an industrial concern, and is in a position to know the character and stability of the house, he may consider the advisability of investing a part of his savings in the stock of the company which employs him; but he should never do this upon the unsupported representation of any officer of his company, however much he may respect that officer and believe in his integrity. It is obvious that an interested official is likely to be biassed. If the stock is worth buying, several first-class banks of deposit will accept it as collateral, and the security it offers is known to financiers and business men who have no interest in it, except that they hold it as an investment. The mere fact that you like your employer does not furnish sufficient reason for buying the industrial stock he represents.

Thousands of industrial corporations have attempted to unload their stock upon their employees, and have appeared to do it as a favor. This is adding hypocrisy to dishonesty.

I again advise the employee to be careful. If the stock is worth buying its value is known, and no reliable man questions it, and somebody besides the officials of the corporation are buying it and holding it.

But no matter how good the stock may be, it is inadvisable to place the whole of one's savings in any one form of investment.

By all means, particularly shun industrial stocks which are advertised with bombastic announcements, and which appear to offer enormous and unusual interest.

I believe that practically all heavily and sensationally advertised industrial stocks are of questionable value, and are, at best, purely speculative; in fact, I feel that most of these companies were incorporated with the intention of unloading upon the public. Probably the business represented is half dead, or dead, the factory old-fashioned and unproductive, and the profit purely prospective. The business used as a basis for issuing the stock may have been profitable at one time, although moderate in volume. It has simply rusted out. Its past record is used as the basis of the advertisements. Its present condition is intentionally forgotten, that the advertisement may announce what has been done, and may appear to guarantee what will be done. If the prospectus is truthful, it tells the truth only in a technical way, and makes the story read well by the presentation of generalities and pasts, and the omission of presents, with zenith-painted pictures of futures.

The stock, then, is likely to have little investment value, and may not have even a speculative one.

The majority of first-class industrial stocks are sold privately, or with modest newspaper advertisements, and the money received is used wholly for development purposes. For example, a woollen manufacturer has succeeded in building up a splendid business. He has every reason to believe that he can materially increase his output. He can do this in two ways: first, by turning in his profits, which will allow him to develop slowly; secondly, he may incorporate his company, or, if incorporated, increase the capital stock. This he places on the market in a dignified way, and the money received from the sale of the stock he uses legitimately for the enlargement of his business. The chances of success are favorable, but may not be sufficiently so to suggest that the stock be purchased by small investors, or by men of moderate income, who had better place their money where the security is at the maximum, or close to it,—in the savings bank, or by the purchase of high-class bonds or mortgages, or of other securities which have a definite intrinsic value,—which are not subject to more than slight fluctuation, and which are not controlled by any one man or small combination of men.

If I may judge from my own experience (and I have personally investigated a very large number of industrial stock propositions), I would say that I look upon the undue and extravagant advertising of an industrial stock as proof positive that it is of little or no value, and that it is not worth anywhere near what is claimed for it. If the company is half as reliable and half as well known as the advertisement states, and if the stock is worth what is claimed for it, it would appear to be easy to raise all the money from, or within, the trade represented, or from conservative speculators, who are willing to take reasonable chances.

So long as money continues to be cheap, and there is so much of it, men with good stock to sell will address their appeals to men of money, and will not go to the great expense of unloading upon the general public.

A fraudulent or questionable stock is heavily advertised, because it cannot be sold to people who are able to measure and weigh it. It must be unloaded upon those who are ignorant of values, and who can be coerced into buying anything which looks well on the face of it.

With billions of money lying idle, and with thousands of capitalists clamoring for investments, it would appear to be obvious that owners of a hundred-thousand-dollar corporation would not go to the expense of putting out from ten to twenty-five thousand dollars in advertising, when their stock, if worth buying, would be handled at a low commission by reputable brokers.

With the small investor, or man of moderate means, who is considering industrial stocks, it is simply a question of whether or not he prefers a high rate of interest with little security, than a low rate of interest with ample security. The fact that industrial stock, or other stock for that matter, is paying a high dividend must not be construed as *prima facie* evidence that this dividend will be continued. Perhaps it is being paid as a bait, so as to attract new stockholders. What is back of the dividends is all-important. If the business is, and has been, successful, if its assets are large, if its profits are at least fair, if it is so organized that the death or disability of one or a few men will not injure it, if it makes and sells a commodity of presumably permanent demand, then the small investor may favorably consider its stock, although I would advise him to give something more solid his preference.

All business is uncertain, especially private business, and no one can guarantee the intrinsic value, or dividend-paying ability, of any industrial stóck.

I am not uncompromisingly advising the small investor against good industrial stocks, but I am simply suggesting to him that there are other forms of investment offering greater security, although at a lower rate of interest.

The large investor, or the man of much money, finds in good industrial stocks a particular and available opportunity for both investment and speculation, but this book is not directed to him. When one becomes wealthy, and can afford to take speculative chances or losses, one is in a position to consider many forms of investment which are not safe for the man of small income to purchase.

Good industrial stocks are thoroughly legitimate, and they are far removed from fraudulent propositions.

In connection with this chapter, however, I would ask the reader to study the one entitled "Fake Investments," not because industrial stock is fraudulent, or even questionable, but because nearly every form of fake investment and opportunity to lose money is some kind of industrial stock, including the always-lose-your-money-quick mining scheme, which frequently does not represent as much as a hole in the ground.

CHAPTER XX

THE REAL ESTATE MORTGAGE

THE mortgage on real estate is, and always has been, considered one of the safest and basic forms of investment, and is used by every class of investors and money-savers, except those who can accumulate but a few hundred dollars. A chattel mortgage is a different affair, and is a lien upon personal property, such as furniture, carriages, and clothing.

A mortgage may be untechnically described as a sort of bill of sale from the mortgagor to the mortgagee, but it differs from the ordinary bill of sale in that the mortgagee's right of possession does not mature until the expiration of the mortgage, provided the interest is paid as agreed upon, and the mortgagor gets back his property unincumbered by returning the money loaned by the mortgagee on the date of the expiration of the mortgage, or before, if the mortgagee will accept it.

Although a mortgage is, in the eyes of the law, a virtual sale or transfer, both the mortgagee and mortgagor are protected each against the other,— the mortgagee, because of the security offered; and the mortgagor, because the sale or actual transfer of his property remains inactive if he pays the interest regularly and the principal at maturity.

The property mortgaged, although in a sense transferred to the lender, is, in practical fact, merely held as security by the mortgagee, who cannot dispose of it, nor remove nor interfere with any part of it, except as specified in the mortgage paper, nor has he any other rights so long as the conditions of the mortgage are lived up to.

The mortgagor may use the property as though he owned it free and clear, subject only to interference on the part of the mortgagee if he abuses, alters, or does anything which will materially lessen the value of the property.

A mortgage on a piece of property is as good as the real estate is, and even better, unless the mortgage covers the full value of the property or is in excess of it.

The mortgagee's rights come before the owner's rights.

If the property is worth more than the face of the mortgage (sufficiently more to provide for depreciation), and the title to it contains no flaw, and the insurance is adequate — provided buildings are included, making insurance necessary

— and the insuring company is sound, then a mortgage is as good, as solid, and as safe an investment as it is possible to obtain, with, perhaps, the exception of United States Government bonds and gild-edged State and city bonds.

The real estate mortgage pays the mortgagee from three to six per cent, occasionally more than six per cent; but any interest above six per cent is obtained at a sacrifice of the best security.

Mortgages on large city properties, including buildings worth several hundreds of thousands of dollars or even millions of dollars, are seldom written at a rate exceeding four per cent, and some of them do not pay over three and one-half per cent. These mortgages are held usually by banks, trust companies, or by large estates. The small investor never figures in them, except indirectly, and has, therefore, little interest in them, save as they represent a security for his deposits in a savings bank or other institution.

The trustees of large properties prefer the strongest security at a necessarily low rate of interest, and the large city mortgage is one of the best investments for them.

Few homestead, farm, or residential mortgages are placed at less than four per cent, the average rate in the East being five per cent, and in the West and South from five to six per cent.

Rates of interest are subject to territorial or financial conditions, the stronger the security the lower the rate of interest. During panics, when much money is temporarily locked up, it may be sold or let out at an exorbitant rate of interest.

No Eastern real estate owner is justified in paying more than five per cent, provided he does not borrow more than sixty or seventy per cent of the selling value of his property. If the property has a fixed value, which does not often occur, he may borrow more than seventy per cent at five per cent. He will pay, usually, five and one-half or six per cent, if he borrows money in advance of building, the payments to be made as the building progresses. This matter I have considered in the chapter entitled "Owning a Home."

Money is worth, usually, a little more in the West and South than it is in the more conservative East; and, therefore, a higher rate of interest is obtainable; but high interest-paying mortgages are not to be recommended to the small investor, salary-receiver, and wage-earner, unless he is thoroughly familiar with the property, and it is considered by conservative investors as offering ample security.

A not always written, and not by any means always followed, savings bank regulation forbids the loan of a larger amount than sixty per cent of the real or selling valuation of the real estate; for example, if a parcel of real estate is worth ten thousand dollars, a savings bank cannot properly loan more than six thousand dollars upon the property. This condition, however, is not by any means lived up to by other than the most conservative and best managed institutions, for others frequently loan money dangerously close to valuation; but as they loan so much, they may not suffer losses which will materially lower the value of the security offered their depositors.

The cheapness of money at certain times and the competition in money-loaning apparently force some of the savings banks, and other conservative investors, to take greater chances than they would permit under normal conditions. But, fortunately, these risks are usually spread out sufficiently to protect the bank against more than occasional loss.

When this practice of loaning as much as eighty or ninety per cent upon property becomes chronic, the transaction is on a plane of speculation; and no bank is safe or sound which practises it.

The assessed valuation of real estate property may not represent its real and selling value, but in the majority of cases, it is under the selling price.

A parcel of real estate has two distinct valuations: first, what it will bring under the hammer, that is, at a forced sale; and, second, what the owner can sell it for within a reasonable time.

It is unfair to appraise an estate at what it will bring at auction, because few properties sell to advantage under the red flag.

No general rule of valuation-making can be made. Judgment is the strongest factor. May I not suggest, however, that it is reasonably safe to consider a piece of property worth what it would probably bring at auction plus half the difference of the price which conservative real estate men believe would be realized upon it if sold under favorable conditions. For example, if the property would probably sell at auction for one thousand dollars, and conservative appraisers believe that it would bring twelve hundred dollars under favorable conditions, it is fair to consider it worth eleven hundred dollars. One can safely loan from sixty to seventy per cent of eleven hundred dollars upon this property, and he should not loan more than sixty per cent of its supposed value, unless the property is very desirably located and appears to be subject to increased valuation.

Real estate men, and all other men for that matter, are likely to be biassed, and it is not well to take the unsupported opinion of any one of them, nor should you consult only buyers and sellers of real estate. The first-class business man, who undoubtedly owns some real estate, is more likely to be fairer in his judgment.

It is difficult to get at rock bottom, but if you loan only sixty per cent of what conservative men consider the true valuation, the transaction is likely to be reasonably safe, for comparatively few pieces of good real estate are likely to drop as much as forty per cent.

Second and third mortgages are subsequent liens upon property, a second mortgage covering it after the first mortgage, and the third mortgage covering the property after the first and second mortgages. They have no value, and offer no security, unless the property is worth more than that of the existing first mortgage or first and second mortgages.

The first mortgagee has all the rights and privileges, and none of these extend to the subsequent mortgagee until the earlier mortgagee is satisfied.

Second and third mortgages are perfectly safe, if the security is ample; but, upon general principles, I would advise the small investor to have nothing to do with them. They should be confined to experienced investors, who are thoroughly familiar with real estate, are able to weigh values to a nicety, and can afford to take speculative chances.

It is obvious that second and third mortgages pay a higher rate of interest than that required by the owner of the first mortgage.

While the first or bottom mortgage offers pretty close to giving the maximum of security, and pays a fair rate of interest, the mortgage is a safe investment only when the property has a tangible or obtainable value, and is not liable to more than slight fluctuation, when the title is clear, and the insurance good. Further, the value of the mortgage is dependent upon its proportionate size compared with the value of the property. A mortgage for more than sixty per cent is not considered positively safe, as mortgages run. Seventy per cent may be fairly safe, and some times even eighty or ninety per cent is not without good security; but the small investor should seldom consider placing his money in a mortgage representing more than sixty per cent of the probable valuation of the property.

A good mortgage is not a speculative proposition. It cannot possibly pay more than the interest specified. The mortgagee is not likely to be able to obtain the property, for if it is worth much more than the face of the mortgage upon it, the mortgagor can prevent foreclosure, and save his property. A good mortgage is, then, simply an investment, and worth its face value, never more or less.

Notwithstanding that the mortgage is theoretically safe, and the low mortgage looks absolutely safe, numerous losses have occurred, due to several causes.

First, the title may not be clear, and may contain one or more flaws, which will invalidate it to the mortgagee's loss; because, if the mortgagor does not own the property free and clear, and without objectionable restrictions, it is obvious that he cannot give the mortgagee a good title to it. A flaw in a title is, however, often cleared at slight expense. Bad titles are not uncommon. No one should place a mortgage until he is assured that the title is sound. This may be ascertained with a reasonable degree of accuracy by a good title-searcher, or the title may be insured by a title insurance company.

Secondly, if the property mortgaged is occupied land, the fire insurance company writing the policy may fail to be able to pay any, or but a small part, of the amount insured. In this case, the mortgagee meets with a loss, as it is probable that the land is not sufficient to cover the mortgage. A fire risk, of course does not operate unless there is perishable property in the form of houses or other buildings. Most of the fire insurance companies are sound, and the insurance policy offers, usually, ample protection against loss by fire.

Thirdly, perhaps the greatest risk in mortgage-taking is in the making of an unsafe loan upon property; that is, the lender loans more money than the value of the property would warrant. The mortgagor misrepresents, intentionally or otherwise, and places an inflated value upon the property, which it may be impossible to detect, unless one is an expert.

In this country there are thousands of mortgages written for amounts larger than the probable valuation of the property mortgaged. There is no law against placing a mortgage upon property in excess of its valuation. I have a perfect legal right to lend a thousand dollars upon a hundred dollars' worth of property, and the mortgage would be duly registered.

Speculators and dishonest real estate brokers frequently make a specialty of dealing in unsafe mortgages. They mortgage property of their own, or held by dummies or middlemen. These mortgages are written for the full valuation, or more than the valuation, of the property. They are entirely legal. They sell them to small investors, and to those who are not able to weigh values. These men also place mortgages upon property which they have for sale, the mortgage representing more than the value of the property, and then attempt to sell it for a small payment down, the mortgage remaining. For example, let us suppose that a piece of property is worth five thousand dollars. The real estate manipulator sells the house to a dummy, taking back a mortgage of about five thousand dollars. He then, apparently, acts as selling agent for his dummy, and offers the alleged equity in the property for five hundred or a thousand dollars. The buyer gives a thousand dollars for the equity, when, in fact, he purchases nothing. He has simply made the agent a present of a thousand dollars.

In buying a piece of mortgaged property, do not consider the mortgage as safe unless it is held by a reliable bank or first-class investor, and even then, subject it to full investigation. Many a man has purchased a home under mortgage, and has for several years made payments on the so-called equity, only to discover that his first dozen payments have been literally placed in the air.

Unless one is experienced in real estate, it is practically impossible to appraise property close to its actual selling valuation. One is more likely to judge superficially, and to value the property from what it appears to be worth at the present time, without taking into consideration future conditions.

It should be obvious that the value of a house, for instance, is dependent upon both the present and future worth of the land upon which it stands. A palace, costing a million dollars to erect, and located in the backwoods, might not sell for more than a thousand dollars, because nobody would want it.

In every country there are situated magnificent residential edifices, costing vast sums of money; and yet comparatively few of them may be sold for more than a small fraction of their cost.

The cost-valuation must not be considered except in close connection with location-valuation. A mortgage of five thousand dollars, upon a summer home costing a hundred thousand dollars, may not be worth more than half of its face value.

Then, environment changes, and sometimes very suddenly. A respectable neighborhood to-day, becomes a disreputable one to-morrow. Land worth one dollar a square foot on a certain street may not bring fifty cents per foot five years from now. The erection of a factory materially injures the selling value of residential property, and a garage built near-by may lower it twenty-five per cent.

It is, however, very unusual for property to depreciate as much as forty per cent within the life of the average mortgage.

Let us suppose, for example, that you loan six thousand dollars upon a ten-thousand-dollar property, the house and land being worth, presumably, ten thousand dollars. At the time of placing the mortgage you have ample present security and probable future security. It is quite likely that the building of a factory near by, or any other condition arising, will not bring the property below the six-thousand-dollar point within five years. If your mortgage does not run for more than this length of time, you are reasonably secure.

In determining the investment value of a piece of real estate, it is, as I have shown, as necessary for you to diagnose its future as well as its present valuation. This is frequently difficult to do. Even the shrewdest real estate manipulators have suffered heavy losses, and many of them have become bankrupt. There is an element of risk in mortgage-taking, although it may not be admitted by all real estate men.

Do not take a mortgage on a house to be built, advancing money as the building progresses, unless the owner of the land is known to be thoroughly honest, and the contractor or builder is a man of integrity. True, the temptation to obtain an additional rate of interest is great, and these mortgages are frequently thoroughly safe. Many residences are erected on these instalment mortgages. The owner has his land free and clear. Let us suppose, for example, that the land is worth a thousand dollars, and that the to-be-erected house will cost five thousand dollars. When the house is completed, the property will be worth six thousand dollars. The owner of the land mortgages his land and his to-be-built house for four thousand dollars, the mortgagee paying over to him, or to his builder, the money in instalments, the mortgagor paying interest upon the entire four thousand dollars, although he may not receive the whole of it for several months. It is easy for the contractor or builder, and for the owner himself, to misrepresent. The mortgagee is not likely to understand thoroughly the building business, and he may pay over his money faster than the building is built, giving the owner and builder an opportunity to put the money into their pockets, and to stop work upon the building, either from dishonest motives or from necessity, and both may use the money for outside speculation, with or without intention of making good.

The only advantage of this kind of a mortgage is that it bears an additional rate of interest.

While I consider the real estate mortgage one of the best forms of investment, I would caution the small investor, salary-receiver, or wage-earner against mortgage-taking, unless he understands the real estate business or has friends who will give him expert and honest advice. However safe the mortgage may be, the money in it is usually tied up, so to speak. It is often difficult to sell a mortgage, or to raise money upon it, at short notice, and without paying a commission or brokerage, even though the mortgage may be gilt-edged.

The man who is able to save only a little money had better be satisfied with the four per cent interest paid him by the sound savings bank and high-class bond, until he has sufficient money to take slight chances.

Where there is little money, and where loss means great disaster, four per cent with safety is better than higher interest with even not far from the minimum of risk.

CHAPTER XXI

THE CHATTEL MORTGAGE

A CHATTEL mortgage is a legal and registered lien on practically every kind and sort of property other than real estate,— usually representing a loan on furniture, pianos, automobiles, horses, carriages, boats, clothing, jewelry, and personal property, the most of which is in use, or has been used, and is, consequently, second-hand. Chattel mortgages are placed, also, upon stock in trade and every class of merchandise.

The property mortgaged may or may not remain with the mortgagor. He is usually allowed to use it, but he cannot transfer it from one place to another without the consent of the mortgagee.

Thousands of men, known as brokers and commercial agents, earn their livelihood by loaning money on this class of security. It is a business in itself, and should be practised only by those who understand it. It offers, with the exception of speculation, the best opportunity for loss, except to those who are able to appraise values and diagnose human nature. It is practically impossible for any one, unless he be an expert from long experience, to appraise correctly the value of personal property; and judges of human nature are limited in number.

Many of the people who borrow on chattel mortgages are unfortunate through no fault of their own. It may be due to unforeseen circumstances, and is often the result of extravagance.

They are transiently, or chronically, hard-pushed; they turn to the chattel mortgage through necessity, often the most urgent necessity. Frequently they are unable to pay the principal or even the interest; consequently the lender has to foreclose.

Unless one is almost completely hard-hearted, and devoid of most of the compassion which is supposed to accompany humanity, he had better keep out of this business. Of course, he has a right to his money, but to get it, it is often necessary for him to cause much mental and physical suffering, which frequently he must inflict upon the innocent and dependent.

Under no condition would I advise the small investor, salary-receiver, or wage-earner, to loan his money, taking a chattel mortgage for security, unless he does it to help a friend, making his act purely a matter of friendship. I am opposed to it for him as a means of investment, for if he goes into it, using it as a receptacle for his savings, he is pretty sure to be the loser.

CHAPTER XXII

THE FAKE INVESTMENT

THERE are several reasons why I do not claim statistical accuracy for the statements I am about to make. The first reason is based upon the impossibility of finding authoritative data. There are facts and tendencies which we see, and which impress us with their prevalence, and yet they cannot be measured by rule or collated by numbers.

I do not think that I will be accused of exaggeration, or of an attempt to appeal sensationally to the reader, if I advance the opinion that more money is lost, and more families are ruined, by the purchase of questionable and fraudulent mining and other stocks than result from any other cause, in business and out of business, except, perhaps, intemperance.

There are now before the public, and there may be for many years, thousands of alleged investment propositions, all of them sensationally advertised, and most of them offering little other than promises to do what cannot be done, and what their promoters know is impossible of accomplishment. They are virtually wholesale or retail separators of the people from their money, and their existence is responsible for an unrealized proportion of people among the great middle class who are in precarious financial circumstances.

Heavy losses, which produce present suffering and affect the protection of the future, probably drive more men and women to the bad, and injure more children by depriving them of the necessities of existence, than does any other factor which comes into our everyday life. A loss of one's savings, which are usually hard-earned and come from protracted labor, a loss which may be accompanied with inability to provide sufficient food, and other bodily necessities, is, I believe, more responsible, directly or indirectly, for the existence and prevalence of crime, than is any other resourceful factor in the whole criminal catalogue.

If this be true, and I have long heard it advanced by sensible men, he who swindles the public and fraudulently obtains the people's money, is more responsible for the birth and life of vice than is he who practises vice.

The seller and promoter of fraudulent investments, who is usually a man of some apparent responsibility, intentionally ruins men and women, and literally spreads disease and poverty. There are no alleviating circumstances in the action of his cursedness. If there were a stronger word than cursedness, I would use it. He has not even the excuse of the degenerate, who commits crime because of uncontrollable passion, or under great mental or physical provocation.

This criminal of alleged respectability deliberately ruins that he may receive what he does not need,— a superabundance of wealth. The law cannot always reach him, and he will continue to exist, and to flourish, so long as both society and the Church refuse to take the trouble to discriminate, and to investigate not only the personal character of their members, but, what is of far more consequence, their business character.

The immoral man, bad though he is, injures few beyond his personal reach; but the fraudulent promoter and business fakir ruin towns-full of people, debauch legislatures, and are a public menace.

Until alleged respectability becomes real respectability, and people forget dying in learning how to live, and take an interest in politics and citizenship, there would appear to be but one way to offset this growing evil, and that is to tell the public the truth about it, that the public may, if it will, no longer rest in the peaceful sleep of ignorance.

The schemes made and promoted by this class of men are complex and cunning. The man of sense and discretion, unless he has studied the subject and has lived close to human nature, may not readily understand how these financial sharks are able to swindle and re-swindle the people. He does not appreciate the standard ignorance and credulity of the public, and probably has not experienced the insane desire to get rich not only quickly, but instantaneously, at the least possible expenditure of time, thought, energy, and money.

So anxious are the people to get something for nothing, or to get much for little, that I believe one could finance a company which would bond itself to pay the running expenses of the national government, by means of a lottery, the lottery to be conducted on the square, and not as fake financial schemes are manipulated.

The gambling-table instinct is still characteristic of our people, and it is being encouraged and abetted by nearly every class of society. The progressive whist party, the bridge table, and the grab bag, on account of their alleged respectability, are doing much to instil into our children the love of chance, and to give them a foretaste of the excitement of gambling. I am inclined to feel that they are doing more harm than that which comes from the pool room or the policy-shop.

Respectable wrong-doing is more treacherous than is any other form of crime.

An ounce of respectable sin weighs more than a pound of police-court criminality.

The tendency of to-day is to get something with the least possible effort and expenditure, to take speculative and gambling chances. With the full knowledge that these conditions exist everywhere, — in the store, in the factory, in the home, and even in the school and Church,— the financial fakir casts his net and pulls in a straining load of foolish fish.

The country is flooded with flaming advertisements of mining and other companies, which appear to offer everything and to guarantee everything, when, as a matter of fact, their guarantees are worth less than the paper upon which they are written, for the paper was worth something before the advertisement was printed upon it. It is obvious that these expensive advertisements, many of them costing thousands of dollars, would not appear if they did not pay, and they would not pay if the people did not read them and buy the things advertised.

One of the most conspicuous swindlers of the day is the so-called mining company, with or without a mine. In many cases its assets consist of superb, but leased, office furniture, well-dressed clerks, and magnificently printed prospectuses. There is usually a legal title, or option, to some land, perhaps a large tract,— enough to make a good appearance upon large-scale maps and serve as the physical basis for imaginary descriptions.

In my opinion, ninety-nine out of every hundred of these heavily advertised companies offer neither investment nor business propositions; because no mines are located on their properties, or else, if mines do actually exist, they are either unprofitable, or are too far removed from the railroad for ore to be handled to advantage. Many of them are located near a well-known and profitable mine, and the promoters claim that this proximity to an ore-bearing district is evidence of marketable ore. This statement is illogical, and could not be borne out in fact. Proximity to an ore-bearing mine may not insure anything more than scattered ore. Good mining territory has its deserts as well as its oases. Ore runs in veins.

The fact that an alleged mine is near a good mine, must not be considered as more than very indirect evidence that the property is ore-bearing.

Occasionally fraudulent companies actually own mines which are capable of producing enormous quantities of good ore; the mines may be genuine, and the quality of the ore be substantiated by reliable analysis; but in most cases these mines are located away from the railroad, where the cost of transportation forbids possible profits.

I recall a promoter who invaded my community, who came to conquer and who conquered. He was of prepossessing appearance, his clothes fitted him, his watch chain was not too large for a gentleman to wear, and the diamond in his scarf-pin was of modest dimension. By appearing to be moderate in his statements, he gave himself a better opportunity to exaggerate. He was well introduced. There are alleged respectable people who would introduce the devil to their daughters if he were in evening dress,— members of that growing class of society who consider a spotless shirt better than a spotless character. He received an audience. He brought with him samples of ore and photographs of his mine, accompanied with authentic assayers' reports. Investigation showed that he did not exaggerate the ore-bearing capacity of his property or the quality of the ore. Hundreds of men, including many who knew enough to know better, were ready to put money into his mine, and would have done so if it had not been for the shrewdness of one of them. He was acquainted with a man who lived within fifty miles of the mine. He wrote to him, giving him full particulars, and requesting telegraphic information. The following message came over the wire:

"Big mine. Lots of ore. Would take train of bald eagles to lug ore to railroad."

Here were both quality and quantity. The promoter did not misrepresent or exaggerate, so far as the ore was concerned. Legally he could substantiate every statement that he had made; but he intentionally forgot to inform the would-be investor that his mine could never become profitable because of its location.

If you will read carefully the prospectus of the average mining scheme, you will find that, while it apparently tells the truth, and appears to guarantee everything, it is legally irresponsible, probably written by an expert who knows how to juggle words, and who has the ability to make nothing read like something, or to make a little seem like a lot.

The prospectus has, as a rule, much more to say about property in general, than about the property owned by the company. It is filled with pictures, which may and may not come from original photographs; it deals more in futures than it does in presents; what it apparently says is opposed to what it actually says; and it does not really say much of anything, although it appears to cover everything. In nine cases out of ten, yes, in nine and nine-tenths cases out of ten, it is a doctored document,— a typographical fool-catcher.

A careful analysis of the average mining proposition would appear to furnish sufficient proof to any sane man, or to any man with half-sense, that there is no basis for investment. But, unfortunately, sane men and men of half-sense, or with even quarter-sense, do not consider these schemes, and take no pains to warn the public against them. They are left, therefore, to the all-fools or half-fools, who, through natural or acquired ignorance, allow avarice to outweigh everything else.

The camera is a very obedient servant, and makes a specialty of being accommodating. It will make a picture of anything you want it to, and, if you treat it well, it will not show discrepancies. Most of the photographs picture action, and are either fixed-up to represent the grossest exaggeration, or else are not taken upon the property owned by the company. A good picture can be made of a very poor thing, if the photographer knows his business; or a good thing belonging to somebody else may be substituted in an advertisement.

An honest, reliable, and high-class mining expert delivered a lecture recently upon mining enterprises. While holding in his hand the prospectuses of three mining companies, each one of which was a superlative example of the printer's art, he said:

"These companies are said to be located in Blanktown. The prospectuses give them an aggregate valuation of five million dollars. They are selling their stock for ten cents a share, and they guarantee that it will be worth a dollar a share within a year. I live in Blanktown. I am mayor of Blanktown. I am president of the Blanktown National Bank. I never heard of one of these companies, and yet I am supposed to know as much about my town as does anybody who lives in it. Blanktown has a population of less than twenty-five hundred, and yet it appears to be possible to hide five million dollars' worth of property so securely that the mayor and the president of the bank have no suspicion of its existence."

It is a fact that much of the mining stock advertised is not worth the printing of the certificates, and I think I may say with safety that practically all heavily advertised stock is either primarily fraudulent and worthless, or is of questionable value.

Many a company pays a dividend, or appears to do so, the dividend coming out of the money paid in for stock. The foolish buyer receives part of his money back in the form of dividends, the dividend not representing the earnings of the company.

It is easy to pay dividends, and even large ones, when the stock is selling rapidly and for enough money to allow a reasonable amount of it to be used for bait. The only dividends good for anything are the earned dividends. Any promoter can pay large dividends, if enough money comes in from the sale of the stock to allow a proportion of it to be used for the purpose. For example, you pay a hundred dollars for stock, and the promoter still makes money if he gives you a dividend of half of it, at the same time dangling the bait of a dividend-paying investment, which you and your friends are eventually sure to bite. In other words, he gives you back half of your hundred dollars, and swindles you out of the balance only, in order to establish confidence.

I have already tried to explain the reasons which permit the fraudulent promoter to prey upon people, and to do it continuously, but the following story illustrates them.

A scheme-promoter and his friend were smoking at the club. Between puffs of fifty-cent cigars, which manipulators can afford to smoke, the following conversation took place:

"Mr. Blank," said the friend, "how under the sun do you manage to unload the stock of your company, when every sensible man knows, and you know, that your property is not worth one per cent of what you claim it is; and you know, and I know, that it can never earn a dividend? It is a fake, pure and simple."

The promoter did not get angry. Promoters never do. Their faces are metal-plated, and their consciences are iron-covered. They are too well satisfied, and making too much money, to be provoked, even at the truth. Throw truth at them, and it does not harm them if it hits them.

"My friend," replied the promoter, "step to the window and count a hundred passersby, and tell me when you reach the hundredth one."

In a few minutes, the required number of people had passed the window, and the friend reported it to the promoter.

"How many of them, my boy," said the promoter, and his eyes twinkled, "how many of the hundred you have just counted really think for themselves? How many of them know anything beyond what they have to know?"

The friend puffed silently, and watched the

rings of smoke ascend and disappear. Then he said:

"I should think about one; possibly a little less than one."

Arising, the promoter slapped his friend upon the back and exclaimed, "I sell my stock to the ninety-nine plus."

Some of the claims and statements made by exploiters are so extravagant, so obviously untrue, so sublimely exaggerated, and often so intensely humorous, and, mark you, so successful as they run, that they furnish indisputable evidence that a proportion of the great middle class of people have brains, judgments, and understandings made up of streaks of sense running parallel to streaks of idiocy.

Recently a projector succeeded in selling considerable stock in a company which either was to operate, or which merely claimed to be going to operate, a cat ranch. The announcement of the company, printed upon coated paper, between illuminated covers, read that the promoter would collect a million net cats. This brilliant statistician and mathematician, basing his diagnostical statements upon the scientific attainments of the ages, assumes, without allowance or reservation of any kind, that each cat would average twelve kittens a year. At the end of the first year there would be on hand a stock of one million original cats plus the cumulative dividend of twelve million kittens or cats,—a net stock of thirteen million cats of diverse ages. The promoter guarantees that he can sell each white skin at ten cents, and each pure black skin at seventy-five cents. His knowledge of the future is so unassailable that he estimates that the twelve million skins will sell at an average of thirty cents apiece, making a revenue of about ten thousand dollars a day gross from cats killed, at the same time reserving one million cats for stocking-up purposes.

The promoter assures the prospective purchaser of stock that one expert man, or that one and a fourth expert women, can skin fifty cats a day at a wage of two dollars. Consequently it will take a hundred men to operate the ranch, giving a net profit of nine thousand eight hundred dollars per day.

He proposes to establish a rat ranch next door, where a good grade of rats will be raised as food for the cats.

Rats multiply four times as fast as cats, therefore one million progressive rats will furnish four rats per day for each cat. This wonderful promoter, who is probably the great grandson of the fellow who tried to discover perpetual motion, has no difficulty in providing for the physical care of the rats, because the carcasses of the cats are not sold with their skins; hence what is left of the cats is eaten by the rats, allowing a fourth of a cat for each rat per day.

It will be seen, even by the dullest investor, that the business cannot help but be self-supporting and automatic. The cats will start in by eating the rats; and the rats, before and after being eaten by the cats, will eat what is left of the cats; and the company will get the skins.

While this idea is not strictly original,— being only a method of realizing financially upon the Kilkenny cat theory,—the promoter fails to carry it far enough, and moreover, shows great biological ignorance, because he does not skin the rats before giving their left-overs to the cats. This waste will undoubtedly be remedied, and will double the value of the stock.

Prospective buyers are earnestly requested to telegraph their orders, otherwise they are not likely to get an opportunity to share in the enormous profits of the concern.

Ridiculous as the foregoing scheme seems to be, the assertions and figures are taken directly, in a condensed form, from an announcement actually sent out to the people, and presumably bringing returns.

There is, and must be, a reason for everything,

and all things permit of logical conclusions. If the property is as valuable as the promoter says it is, do you think there would be any need of such strenuous pushing for the selling of the stock?

Our financial centres are flooded with idle money. Money is plenty and cheap. Is it at all likely that the owner of a really good proposition would find much difficulty in raising the necessary funds for its development from the men who have money and who are anxious to invest it? Would extensive advertising and elaborate prospectuses be used, if there were sufficient intrinsic value to speak for itself without the flaring of typographical banners? Would the promoter sell stock for less than what it is worth, if it was worth what he says it is worth?

No. The promoter advertises that he may reach the fools, because the fools will buy anything.

It may not be generally known that the great miners of the country employ a class of employees, known as "detective workmen," each one being an experienced miner. When a new mine is discovered, and trained miners have some reason to believe that there is something in it, these detective workmen obtain positions there as working miners. They easily discover the worth of the mine. They report to their employers. If what they say is favorable, regular mining investors, men who know how to weigh mining values, buy up the mine or become interested in it, and the stock is seldom if ever advertised more than moderately.

The great mining interests of America are able to take care of all the good mines, and these mines are not likely to be offered to the public at less than par.

I think that we may set it down as a fact that practically all mining stock advertised at less than par is worth nothing, or very little, and that it is in every respect an unsafe investment.

So far as my experience and investigation go, I declare emphatically, and without qualification, that I never knew of a profitable or valuable mining stock, or any other kind of stock, which was offered at a few cents on the dollar or was more than moderately advertised.

I consider the heavy advertising of stock at below par, or extensive advertising of any stock, as reasonable evidence of probable fraud.

Further, I would advise every investor to keep away from any stock, where the advertisement of it announces that the price will be raised within thirty days, or within any other specified time.

Legitimate stocks rise or fall because of the

demand or lack of demand for them, as well as by their intrinsic value, and the date of this change cannot be set by any financier, or by anybody else, for nobody can foresee the future value of any stock. If the stock is going to be worth much more in thirty days, is it not obvious that the promoter himself, or his friends, would purchase the whole of it, and not be philanthropic enough to accommodate the public by allowing it to come in?

I would advise every investor to shun any kind of stock or investment the announcement of which suggests philanthropy or the desire to benefit the public. I believe that any statement in an advertisement to the effect that the promoter wants to do good, to share his profits with the customer, is *prima facie* evidence of intentional, premeditated fraud.

Further, I consider any statement to the effect that a limited number of shares will be sold to one person as of fraudulent intent, and should be so considered.

Business is business, and there is no sentiment about it. The seller sells, because he wants to sell, and he cares nothing about the buyer.

Keep away from any company which claims to let you in on the ground floor. This position is occupied by the promoters, and the public is lucky if it gets on to the roof,— unlucky, rather, because it is likely to take a tumble.

Upon general principles, it is well not to purchase any advertised investment, unless the advertisement is moderate in tone, is small in size, and bears the signature of a thoroughly reliable banking house.

Before investing in mining, or in any other stock, I advise you to protect yourself by investigating along the following lines:

In the first place, look up the reputation and standing of the promoters and others connected with the company. Probably most of them are unknown or little known, and a close investigation may show that some of them have been under indictment and have figured in the criminal courts.

Occasionally, the names of good men appear in the announcement. This is often accomplished, because many men of character are ignorant of business ways, and are, therefore, an easy prey to smooth-tongued and broadcloth-clad adventurers.

Occasionally, you will find the name of a leading divine in the company's directory. Probably he is sincere, and has been led into doing that which he would not have done had he known the truth.

I would advise you to beware of any announcement containing the names of clergymen, doctors, or other professional men, no matter how honest they may be. As they are not good business men, they may have been inveigled into allowing the use of their names. The very appearance of their names may be considered an evidence of fraud. Their innocence and ignorance do not offer you any protection.

Carefully analyze the names of the officers and directors. Some of them may be billed as follows: "John Blank, of the great firm of John Blank and Company." It may have but a bare existence.

The fact that one of the directors is the president of a bank is insignificant, unless the bank is of high financial standing.

There are many banks and trust companies, which are unworthy of public confidence, and are but accessories to swindling schemes.

Positively refuse to invest in any stock unless the company is officered by men of solid reputation, men of unquestionable character, men whose reputations are above par. But even then I would advise you to be cautious. You have no right to take speculative chances, unless you are a professional investor.

Before purchasing mining or other kinds of stock, I suggest that you call upon the president and cashier of several reliable banks or institutions for savings. Request these men to read the prospectus issued by the company, and ask them for information regarding the stock as an investment. If all of them, or most of them, speak highly of it, then you will have some justification for purchasing it; but I would advise you to drop it, if even one of these men condemns it.

Give no weight to the financial opinion of any professional man, unless he has a reputation for financial sagacity. Rather depend upon the advice of business men, and do not allow any one business man to settle the matter for you.

If an investment is good for anything, there are, at least, half a dozen first-class business men, who will not only advise you to buy the stock, but who have purchased it themselves for investment.

Pay absolutely no attention to any claim made by a promoter. Purchase nothing unless several business men of character and standing would, without qualification, advise you to make the investment.

But be careful not to interview people who are friendly to the stock, because they may be indirectly in the employ of the promoter. A little investigation may show that the stock is selling on the street at a much lower rate than that asked for it at the company's office.

Think a little. How many people do you know

who have made a cent by buying mining stock or other advertised investments? I am not referring to the names given in the gilt-edged prospectuses. How many people do you actually know, directly or indirectly, who would repeat their experiments in stock-buying?

The buying and selling of stock belongs to financiers, to men who can afford to lose, and who are able to take speculative chances. Even if the opportunities of success were a dozen times greater than they are, I would advise the small investor to keep away from stocks as they run.

Allow your good sense to rise to the surface and to take command of your pocket-book. Suppress enough of your folly,— for you must have some, as none of us are without it,— to hold your money in safe keeping.

Even the crudest common sense knows, or should know, that, if the stock is as good as the promoter reports it to be, it would not be sold for a few cents on the dollar or at bargain prices, when the safe deposit boxes of the world are overflowing with unused money.

If the mine owner has not sufficient money to develop his mine, and his mine is a good one, would it not be more profitable to obtain money where money is cheap, from men of money, men who know how to manipulate money, than it would be to spend thousands, and hundreds of thousands, of dollars in advertising the stock and for extravagance in selling?

Another good way to find whether or not the stock is good for anything is to ask the promoter to give you the names and addresses of those who have purchased the stock three, six, or nine months previously. Visit these people, or correspond with them. Find out whether or not they are ready to sell, and, also, whether or not they would buy any more stock at the present prices.

As the man without friends is hardly a man, so the investment without high-class recommendations is unsafe and unworthy of consideration.

Still another excellent way to test the investment value of any stock, or other security, is to ask the president, cashier, or other official of a conservative bank, to loan money upon it; that is, ask him if he will take this stock as collateral either at eighty per cent of its par value, or at a much lower per cent. No stock is worth buying, to hold as an investment, unless leading bankers will receive it as collateral for at least seventy-five per cent of its face value.

Still another good way of testing is to call at, or write to, the promoter's office and ascertain the selling price of the stock, then, under the name of a friend, ask this same promoter what he will give you for a certain number of shares of the stock. Let us suppose, for example, that the stock is offered at ten cents a share, and that the promoter states positively that it will be worth a dollar a share within a year. If this be the case, it is obvious that financiers would buy up the entire issue, and that the promoter would gladly buy back the stock at a price very little less than the selling price. Try him and see, and the chances are that he would not pay you one cent a share for the stock he is selling you at ten cents a share, unless he knew you were making the test, and purchased a few shares for advertising purposes.

Under the chapter heading of "Industrial Stock," I have attempted to warn the reader against another important class of fraudulent investment. Every kind of property, and every class of business, is dishonestly promoted by swindlers, but the majority of questionable and dishonest companies handle mining, oil, land, and industrial properties, largely because, perhaps, these kinds of property lend themselves to highly colored descriptions and greatly exaggerated statements.

True, the savings bank and the bond pay a very low rate of interest, but sure little interest is worth more than unpaid great interest. Better receive little interest, than risk your principal for big interest.

"When in doubt, don't," is a pretty safe rule to follow.

CHAPTER XXIII

OWNING A HOME

THE chronic materialist labors under his self-generated delusion that there can be no home worth having, unless the occupants of it hold clear title to the purely material part of it. He has a tumultous feeling of grief-showing-sympathy for the flat-dweller and boarding-house inmate. Upon the lecture platform, if he be an educator, or upon the stump, if he be a politician, he tells the people that the strength and integrity of the nation are vested in the home-houses of its people. He has forbidden the millennial sun to peep over the earthly horizon until every family is separately housed and owns a piece of land with a building upon it.

While I would not minimize the intrinsic value of the material home, and the paid-for home-house, while I believe that one is far better off with a home of his own, and while I feel assured that separate houses are preferable to collective abodes like flats and boarding-houses, I am not willing, as yet, to bring myself close enough to earth to refuse to believe, and to feel, that the true home is as much of a spiritual and mental affair as it is materialistic, and that it is not, therefore, necessarily, wholly dependent upon physical conditions or environment. Undoubtedly the combination of the right kind of spiritual home with the material house produces a far better result than either can hope to offer by itself alone.

The home-making spirit, even though it may be manifested in the materialistic, is to be encouraged by Nation and State, and by every individual who would help the present and provide for the future.

Probably the healthiest and best material form of a home is a detached house, with its own independent yard, provided that sanitary and other necessary conditions are satisfactory. It is obvious that this kind of a residence cannot exist in the heart of a great city, but must be located in either the suburbs or the country. It is a fact, unfortunately, that business and livelihood-earning conditions force millions of people to live in large cities, and will not permit them to visit the country except at occasional intervals.

There appears to be no good reason why every one should not strive to own and occupy, or to occupy without owning, a separate and independent house and yard, provided that they are not off-set by inevitable disadvantages, by local conditions, and by distance and travel.

Fathers and mothers have rights, and all of these rights should not be always sacrificed for the children. Where sacrifice is necessary, it should be divided up among all the members of the family, that it may not fall wholly upon any one of them, except where there is sickness or constitutional weakness.

Although I am opposed to the bringing up of children in the city flat, or in any other closed-in apartment, I have little sympathy with the sentimentalist, who would drive the hard-working father into the distant suburbs or country, with poor transportation facilities, when his work requires his early and late presence in the city. The health of the bread-earner is as necessary as the health of the children, and both should be considered.

Bad as the city flat is, it is better for some people, and some families, than is the suburban home,— not better in itself, but better because of peculiar and unfortunate circumstances.

City life has some advantages, and the flat-dweller can often die of old age, if he will. One can be healthy almost anywhere, if one takes proper care of oneself. Attention to personal matters is as important as satisfactory environment. The healthiness of the open country is often over-estimated. City water, polluted though it may be, is purer than that coming from the average country well. The sanitary conditions in the city are usually better than those in the open country. The city man is nearer his work. It is better, therefore, for some men to be flat-dwellers, provided they can reside in a respectable part of the city, than it is for them to spend a large portion of their time in uninteresting travel, always in crowded and poorly ventilated cars, and invariably at the sacrifice of time and comfort.

But I would enthusiastically recommend the suburban or country home-house, or even the suburban flat, to those who can maintain it, because, upon general principles, the country, and especially the open country, is preferable to the city block and street, and certainly the country is the place for children.

But do not forget that your family can thrive almost anywhere, if they take the proper care of their physical bodies. Care of the body has much more to do with health than mere surroundings. Folk live and die in every community, and under all conditions. But give the suburbs or the country the preference.

It is obvious that the city man of small income cannot own either a flat or a city residence. If he would have a home-house of his own, he must locate in the suburbs or in the country. It is also obvious that the young married man especially does not have the ready cash for the full purchase of a modest home. He must either wait a considerable time, or obtain his house and land on mortgage.

Is it better to wait until one is able to own a home of his own, or to live in a mortgaged house? Whichever way may be preferable, it is a fact that probably ninety-five per cent of the residences in the city or near the city, and that fully sixty per cent of the country homes, are either under mortgage or were obtained with the aid of a mortgage. So universal is this custom, that it would be difficult to argue against mortgaged home-houses.

Economists of every class, and most of our leading philanthropists, are almost unanimously agreed that it is better to have a home-house that is mortgaged than no home-house at all, provided the cost of carrying the mortgage is not burdensome.

It is easy to place upon a house a mortgage of from sixty to seventy-five per cent of its real or selling value, and savings banks, or other conservative money-lending institutions, are looking for chances to lend money on good real estate, never realizing a rate of interest over six per cent, and usually only five per cent, if the security is satisfactory.

In New England, and other parts of the East, money can be had at five per cent, six per cent being required in some Western and Southern localities.

Let us suppose, for example, that a man, with a family and a fair income, has sufficient money to pay from thirty to forty per cent of the cost of a house and land. Most assuredly would I advise him to make the purchase of this home-house, allowing a mortgage not exceeding seventy per cent to be placed upon it. I would prefer a mortgage of not over sixty per cent, provided, of course, that the owner intends to remain permanently in town, and that the location selected is not likely to deteriorate in value.

I do not advise any one to submit himself to a mortgage so large that he has no real equity in the property.

While the manipulation of real estate, next to the practice of agriculture, is said to be the basis of wealth-getting, real estate, both good and bad, cannot usually be disposed of at will. It is not negotiable like a bond or a share of high-class stock, nor is it easy to let a house to a good tenant. Many a desirable place has remained vacant for months and years, and from ten to twenty per cent of the people who hire houses either pay slowly or do not pay at all.

I would recommend most emphatically the purchase of a home-house to any one with a family, or with a prospective family, provided he is permanently located, and is able to assume the responsibility. It is certainly a good way to invest one's money, and the money remains where he can see it, feel it, and live with it. It encourages thrift, and adds to character and stability.

Hundreds of thousands of families are living in houses obtained under the instalment payment plan. Each month they make a payment of an amount which may not be much more than the regular rent would be. This money reverts to the principal, so that when all of it has been paid, they will have a clear title to the property, or an arrangement may be made whereby a deed will be given after a certain number of payments have been made, the balance to be held on mortgage. This is an excellent way to obtain a home-house, provided one is reasonably sure that he can meet his obligations; but it never should be taken advantage of by those whose incomes are both small and intermittent; nor should this arrangement be entered into under any forfeiture clause in the agreement which forfeits to the purchaser all the money he has paid in if he does not make all of his payments.

So popular has become this method of obtaining a home that it has been taken advantage of by land speculators and land sharks, who have been able, by extensive advertising, and by every form of misrepresentation, to swindle the public out of millions of dollars. They usually purchase cheap land in the vicinity of good land. A very attractive plan is drawn, with modern streets laid out, and all necessary improvements. Many of these streets and improvements remain upon paper. Lots are sold at an apparently low price, and upon instalments, often a sum as small as five dollars being sufficient for the first payment. Then the land manipulator offers to build a house at a stated price, which is almost invariably more than the house is worth. He makes the proposition attractive by offering to sell it on what he calls easy terms. The man of moderate income jumps at the bait, and because he can afford to pay a few dollars a month, he eventually finds himself obligated to either lose what he has paid in or pay from twenty-five to fifty per cent more than the property is worth.

The principle of instalment home-buying is thoroughly legitimate, and certainly offers many advantages to the salary-receiver or wage-earner, provided he keeps away from land schemes, from boomed land, and avoids all property which is not well located.

I would advise him to have nothing whatever to do with over-advertised property, with land boomers of any class, unless the property is thought well of by conservative real estate men who have no interest in it.

Never buy any real estate, vacant land, or land with a house on it, until you have consulted at least two first-class business men, who are real estate owners, and who are able to appraise real estate. Never take the unsupported word of the man who has the real estate to sell. Officers of savings banks are usually well posted upon real estate matters.

Many people build their houses, borrowing the money in advance of the erection of the building. They own the land free and clear, and the borrowed money is paid over to them as the building progresses. Under this arrangement they pay interest on the whole amount borrowed, or to be borrowed, even though the building may not be completed for several months. Usually they pay one per cent more interest, because the loaner takes a greater risk. I am not advising against this plan. It has its advantages, and is frequently the best way to obtain a home-house.

While I am very much opposed to indebtedness, and while I believe that a man who is free and clear has a better chance to fight the battle of life, I feel reasonably sure that the home-house, with a mortgage upon it, is better than no home-house at all.

A mortgage of fair size on a piece of property, which the mortgagor can handle without undue pressure, need not be, and should not be, a stumbling block in the way of success-making. It gives him the opportunity of maintaining a home of his own, and this should be an incentive to save.

There are few better or safer ways for the investment of money than to place it in a home-house, provided the location and other conditions are right.

When one has his money invested on his own premises, he sleeps upon his investment,— he derives a benefit from it other than financial. But let him be careful. Better be overcautious than hasty. If the location is not good, or if it is likely to deteriorate, his investment may be a very poor one and entail considerable loss. Changes are always occurring and many a good location has become a poor one within a few years. A good neighborhood cannot be guaranteed. The erection of a garage, or of a factory, near by, may injure the adjoining property sufficiently to wipe out the equity held by the owner.

The value of real estate is dependent upon its location and the adjoining property, and the worth of the building is dependent as much upon its location as upon the cost of its construction; for example, a brick business block, costing one hundred thousand dollars and located in a purely residential district, would not be worth anywhere near as much as it would be if on a business street. A ten-thousand-dollar residence, in a small village, would not sell for much more in the open market than would a house costing half that amount. A palace in the wilderness may not be worth any more in dollars and cents than is the hermit's camp on the other side of the hill. What you pay for building a house does not necessarily fix its value, for the location of the house has much to do with it.

In purchasing a home-house, then, you should consider, not only the cost of construction, but the present and future value of the location.

While I would advise a man of family, or of other dependents, to purchase a home, or equity in one, provided he can afford the expense, and his income is well assured, I would not advise him to put all of his money into real estate, either for a home or for an investment.

It is not good judgment to put your last dollar, or near your last dollar, into any piece of property, for it will leave you without ready funds, and it is not safe to be without ready money.

Let us suppose, for example, that you can afford to carry a three-thousand-dollar home-house. If you have only one thousand dollars available cash, and it is necessary for you to use the whole of this money for the first payment, I would advise you to wait; but if you have from fifteen hundred to two thousand dollars in cash, you are probably in a position to put a thousand dollars into a home-house, the balance of your money to be kept where it will be available. For the man of family should carry some ready cash to meet emergencies, and he should never lock up all of his money where it cannot be easily and quickly realized upon.

No matter how much your equity may be in the house itself, it is difficult to raise money upon mortgaged property without paying a premium and without considerable delay. Cash in hand is the only thing that will meet emergencies, unless one has much property or extensive credit. Better be without a home-house than without ready money.

Again, let me impress upon you the necessity

of making a full investigation of the locality, and of other conditions, before purchasing any real estate, and, further, have the title carefully examined by a good lawyer, or guaranteed by an insurance company.

Hundreds and thousands of people have lost their all by purchasing home-houses, and other real estate, because of unforeseen depreciation and bad titles. Of course, certainty is impossible, and we must take some chances; but intelligent and persistent investigation is likely to prevent loss.

Do not depend upon yourself. Unless you are in the real estate business, or own considerable real estate, you cannot possibly be able to appraise property with much accuracy. Consult those who know but who are not financially interested, and do not depend upon the advice of any one man.

Do not imagine that the ownership of a home-house is going to make a success of you. The elements of success-making are composite. The home helps, and so do all other right conditions. You are better off without a home-house than with one when you cannot afford to have one; but the right kind of a man will create a happy and profitable home anywhere and under all conditions.

Owning a Home

The home spirit in a flat is worth more than the lack of it in a palace.

The home of good cheer and good will, located on the upper floor of a dingy city block, is far better, and contributes more to the up-building of man, than does the loveless house resting in a garden of roses.

The man and the woman, not the house, make the home.

CHAPTER XXIV

LIFE INSURANCE

ALTHOUGH the question of life insurance is one of mighty consequence, opinions about it show the greatest diversity, and are continuously subjected to periodical change; therefore, it is well to burn our bridges of prejudice, that we may look upon life insurance as a definite and necessary commodity, and recognize it as a means of protection, possessing its own peculiar and exclusive advantages.

The past and present investigations of life insurance companies, and the many scandals and irregularities which have been unearthed, have turned the searchlight of truth upon one of the largest of our commercial enterprises.

Probably nothing in business, and representative of everyday life, has been subjected to so much comment and criticism, both for and against it; but even the most bitter enemies of life insurance, or rather of the methods followed by life insurance companies, find themselves forced to admit that, if life insurance had not earned a rightful place in the economy of home and business affairs, if it did not possess in large measure the essentials of a commodity, if there were not well-founded reasons for its existence, it would not have reached its present magnitude, nor could it occupy a substantial and permanent place in the world of business.

Its survival, after every fair and unfair attack upon it, has proved it to be a commodity. If it were not, it would have died long ago.

Life insurance, stripped of its technicality, is a very simple proposition. The insurance company or corporation, working under State charter and supposed to be subject to State law, enters into a contract with the insured party, which agreement, in consideration of a cash payment down and a series of cash payments extending over a period of years or during the life of the insured, guarantees to pay the person or persons designated a stated sum of money, either at the death of the insured or at a specified time appearing in the policy.

There are almost innumerable forms of policies, known by various names, such as the so-called "straight life insurance," "endowment insurance," "ten- or twenty-payment life insurance," and insurance written in the form of bonds.

The common or usual form of policy is what is known as "straight life insurance," where one must die to win; although some companies will pay the insured the face value of his straight life policy if he lives to reach an abnormal age.

Another popular form is what is known as endowment insurance. This usually costs double what is paid for a straight life policy. Under this agreement, the company obligates itself to pay the insured the full value of the policy at the expiration of a specified time, or at his death.

The so-called ten-, fifteen-, or twenty-payment policy is a sort of compromise between the straight life and endowment policies, the insured having a paid-up policy after he makes the number of payments called for, but the money not being paid over until his death.

The insurance bond is another form of insurance, the bond having a certain definite value, and being negotiable at face value, and at any time.

All of the States either regulate, or claim to regulate, by law, the forms of policies written within their jurisdiction, and most of the States require the company to write into every policy cash-values, which are operative after the first, second, or third year, which amounts net are due the policy holder if he discontinues payments upon the policy, or desires to cash it in.

I would emphatically advise no one to take out any policy, of any amount whatever, in any company, no matter how strong it may be, unless there is written in the policy definite cash surrender values. If your insurance agent cannot, or will not, place you in one of these companies, consult another agent.

Life insurance is commercially legitimate, and custom and necessity have made it a commodity. If one looks at it through the narrow lens of the purely ethical, he may consider it more or less of a gamble, the insurance company betting on the life of the insured, and agreeing to pay the debt if it loses; but even this severe critic must admit that it differs materially from common gambling, because the insured party continues to contribute to the insurance pool, making his contributions in the form of periodical payments. Nor does the insured need to take lottery or gambling chances, for the good policy has a cash surrender value, and the insured, after a few years, may at any time, receive a benefit other than that coming from luck.

I have said that life insurance is considered a commercial commodity, a business necessity, and a family protection. Commercially it is, but not theoretically, because a commodity, under a strict definition of the term, is something which is not written upon paper, something neither promised nor guessed at, something which is material and weighable, something which we can see and feel. But to all intents and purposes we may consider life insurance a commodity, because it gives us protection, and appears to be necessary under the present social and economic conditions.

The expense of insurance cannot be calculated with complete accuracy, as can be the cost of an eatable or of a house. When you purchase a building, for example, you may be able to determine, by examination, what it is worth; and if you build, you may know what it will cost you. On the other hand, when you take out a life insurance policy you do not know, and cannot know, what the expense of it will be to you, nor does the company know, for neither of you knows how long you will live.

While I recognize the necessity of life insurance, truth compels me to say that I believe the present life insurance policy costs more than does any other commodity. Investigations show that larger commissions are paid by life insurance companies to their agents for the sale of life insurance than are probably given for any other business transaction. Anywhere up to half, or even a larger proportion, of the first payment upon a policy goes to the agent and not to the company, and is not used to increase the company's assets or to give better protection to the policy holder. Instead, it finds its way into the pocket of the agent, the insured party actually paying the agent for soliciting his insurance,—that is to say, we, the insured, pay a proportion of the cost of our insurance, not to the company which insures us, but to the agent who solicits us, and this go-between is without responsibility or reliability, and has no part in the transaction save that of soliciting the business. Even part of our subsequent payments may be given to him.

This condition makes life insurance expensive, forcing it to cost more than economy would justify.

The real, or apparent, necessity for this solicitor, the high commission paid him, when insurance is admitted to have a tangible value, represents one of those peculiar conditions in business-doing, for the existence of which there would seem to be no sensible reason.

So long as we need coaxers, instead of waiters, of trade, commissions or salaries must be paid to the salesmen; but it is extremely difficult to understand why companies find it necessary to give such large commissions for insurance-getting. It would seem that, if we need life insurance, we would have sense enough to walk into the office of an insurance company and buy a policy over the counter, the same as we purchase furniture or clothing; and yet, a representative of one of our largest insurance companies informs me that a voluntary application for life insurance is practically unknown, substantially all policies being written after solicitation, usually with much solicitation, and sometimes virtually with coercion.

Unbiassed men and business economists, who have made a study of the life insurance question, are of the opinion that this form of insurance can be sold for much less than the price charged for it by the insurance companies. This suggests the general establishment of insurance companies under the direction of the State or National Government.

Already savings banks have added insurance departments, and are offering insurance at a fair rate, but not at as low a rate as was expected.

The savings bank is supposed to handle it at cost for the benefit of the insured, and when savings bank insurance becomes general, the expense of carrying a policy will undoubtedly be much less than the cost now prevailing. Certainly an article so vital as good life insurance should not be so largely in the hands of manipulators and financiers, who are in business for the revenue only.

Some form of cheap, and yet thoroughly protective, insurance should be given to the poor and to those of moderate means; and I believe it is the business of the State, if not of the National, Government, to establish and maintain insurance companies at cost.

Life insurance has a value, especially, to three classes of people:

First, the working man, or business man, or clerk of small income, who has, or may have, some one dependent upon him. The uncertainty of life makes it obligatory that he should provide for emergencies and death. Even at an exorbitant cost he is justified in carrying a moderate amount of life insurance, not as an investment, but as a protection. He should purchase the cheapest form of policy, and should not consider any endowment or other form which the insurance company presents as an investment, unless he be a spendthrift and not willing to save except under compulsion.

The second class that can use insurance to advantage includes men of considerable wealth, who live extravagantly and luxuriously, and who are likely, at any time, to meet with financial disaster. They can afford to pay high rates for protection, and life insurance to them may be considered as a sort of investment, which would be questionable under ordinary circumstances. As their incomes are large, they can afford to carry policies representing hundreds of thousands of dollars, and the endowment form gives them a sort of high-class investment, which, under the circumstances, it may not be unwise for them to carry. But I would not advise any conservative man of much money to use the endowment or any other form of life insurance as a pure investment.

The third class of people, who should carry insurance, is the spendthrift, natural born fool, or one who has acquired foolishness,— that class of our population which has little realization of the value of money, and which cannot, or will not, save by any legitimate or systematic method, except where loss accruing from non-payment is great enough to penetrate their understanding. These men have not brains enough, nor character enough, to save systematically. If they lived within a nest of savings banks, they would patronize none of them. If they are frugal to-day, they are criminally extravagant to-morrow. The straight life policy, or even an endowment, may force them to do what they have not sense enough to do voluntarily. Of course, they over-pay for what they get, but they had better over-pay for insurance than for things of less consequence.

There is a large distinction between protection and investment. Life insurance has a protective value, and is often a necessity; but it offers little in the way of investment compared with the ordinary forms of investment. I say this notwithstanding the claims made by insurance companies and the bombastic advertising put out by them.

As all commercial insurance companies are purely business propositions and institutions for money-making, the managers of some of them are likely to exaggerate the truth, and to attempt to force upon the public policies which pay the companies the best, rather than those which are best for the policy holders. They employ highly paid agents, and use methods of coercion as well as of persuasion. Many of them are extravagantly run, pay their officers salaries which are all out of proportion to the amount of work given, and are dishonestly connected with financial institutions, their money being a part of a circle of money, a convenient way of getting money for the putting through of large financial deals. Yet, although not all of the companies are conducted along what may be considered commercial lines of straight honesty, most of them are thoroughly reliable so far as making payments are concerned. They give the protection they claim to give.

So-called industrial insurance at times offers a needed protection even though many economists give it a general condemnation on account of its cost, which they consider exorbitant. I would not advise any one to consider this class of protection until he has consulted some good banker, financier, or business man of standing, telling him frankly of conditions and family responsibilities, and at the same time showing him the kind of policy which he contemplates taking out. There are many forms of this class of insurance, and some of them forfeit to the insured all of his payments if he lapses at any time. I am emphatically against any form of forfeiture policy.

Philanthropists are considering this proposition, and it is to be hoped that the States will, sooner or later, establish industrial insurance departments, which will give needed protection at a much lower cost, and which will not require the insured to forfeit all he has paid if he discontinues his payments.

I would advise a man of small income to consider insurance only as a protection, and not to be influenced by any statement made by the insurance company or the insurance agent. I believe that a proportion of the printed claims made by insurance companies, and especially those so glibly talked by the insurance agent, although sometimes technically true, are almost invariably misleading, and are often intended to deceive.

I think that many an insurance agent writes

a policy under false pretences; but, notwithstanding this condition, and notwithstanding the unreliability, and even rascality, of some insurance men, straight life insurance, for a man of small income, is to be encouraged, and would appear to be a necessity, if any are dependent upon him.

If the family needs protection, and the head of it is not well-to-do, with money securely invested, he should take out a straight life insurance policy as large as he can conveniently carry, as large as he can afford to pay for at the present time and during the probable future. But I advise him not to consider life insurance as an investment. If he has money to invest, after he has properly protected his family by insurance, let him put it in the savings banks, or secure it in some other way. Life insurance is to him a commodity, and he should buy it at the lowest cost.

Remember that it is the company, not the agent, that gives the protection, that the agent has no responsibility whatever.

If you do not know about life insurance, ask some one who does. Obtain the advice of some good business man, provided he is not connected with an insurance company. The officer of your bank is posted, and so are successful men in general.

Avoid all insurance clubs and insurance

schemes. Refuse to believe any statement made in print, or elsewhere, to the effect that there is any club or individual working in your interest. I believe that every one of these clubs, and all of these men, and all so-called insurance experts, are in the employ of some insurance company.

Positively refuse to consider statements made by insurance companies that a certain form of insurance policy gives you a better investment and at less cost than you would receive at a savings bank. Take this statement to a first-class mathematician or accountant, who will undoubtedly make it plain to you that money deposited in a savings bank will give you more than will come from the same amount of money paid to an insurance company. But this condition does not operate against the value of an insurance policy, because life insurance gives a protection against death, and one which should not be ignored by the man of family. But protection is not necessarily investment.

It is true that in some forms of policies you do not pay in the face value of the policy, and that you receive, at its expiration, more money than you gave the company; but if you had put these instalments in the savings bank you would have more money in the bank at the end of ten or twenty years than the face value of your policy.

Bear in mind that policies in all good companies are substantially alike, that there is more apparent than real difference in the forms presented, although each company may use different kinds to catch the unwary. No one good policy is likely to be worth more than another good policy, notwithstanding what the agent says.

The special inducements offered by some life insurance companies, are, in my opinion, purely imaginary, and are used to fool the people.

Select some first-class life insurance company, through the advice of your bank, or some competent friend who is fair and unbiassed, and have as much insurance as you can afford to carry and need for protection.

Read your policy carefully, and if you do not understand it, have it read by some first-class business man or lawyer. It may appear to give you what it does not. Insist upon having inserted the nonforfeiture clause, which prevents the company from taking advantage of any technicality or statement made by you after a year or so has elapsed.

Then, with your policy filed safely away, you will have the comfort of feeling that you have a post-mortem asset whether or not you live to benefit from it.

CHAPTER XXV

FIRE INSURANCE

A DISCUSSION of fire insurance is not out of place in a book like this, because, although it may not be considered a form of regular investment, it is not removed from the investment class, and, certainly, no sharp line should be drawn between pure investment and necessary protection.

The cost of carrying fire insurance is not excessive.

A fire insurance policy should be placed upon every piece of property, which is subject to any risk and can be covered by insurance, including buildings, horses, carriages, automobiles, boats, furniture, works of art, jewelry, and clothing.

So much do I believe in the necessity of fire insurance that I consider an unwillingness on the part of any one properly to protect his property as close to an inexcusable crime. Even if one has only a few dollars' worth of property, he should insure it against loss by fire. The cost is very small in proportion to the value of the protection given.

There are a number of large fire insurance

companies, and most of them are progressive, sound, and reliable.

No first-class agency will write a policy in a weak company, but it is well for you to ascertain the standing of the company before taking a policy in it. It is a deplorable fact that most business men insure in any company presented to them, and that comparatively few of them discriminate for or against a company.

Many insurance agents carry their business in their hats, and do not have even a local standing. They may represent weak and almost worthless companies. If the agent is not a man of standing, refuse to insure in his companies, unless you are assured of their reliability by some first-class business man who is able to weigh insurance values. The character of the agent, however, does not affect the value of the policy. The agent has no responsibility.

Never allow an insurance policy to lapse. Every one should carry a diary, or dated memorandum book, and mention of the expiration of the policy should be placed therein on the date of the expiration, and also on a date a week or more in advance of it.

If you have good local standing and employ a reliable agent, he will, at your request, give you a letter in which he agrees to renew your policy without notice. This fully protects you. If the agent does not officially renew the policy, his agreement to do so amounts to the same thing in law.

It is well to read your policy over carefully. There are many different forms, each one presenting different conditions. Some policies do not cover damage resulting from lightning unless fire occurs. Other policies do not allow you to vacate the premises. Some policies are invalid if you carry more than a gallon of gasoline in your house. Full protection costs very little if any more than partial protection. Make a truthful statement to your agent, and tell him that you want full protection. There is only one price, which is made by the board of underwriters. Consequently, insurance in the strongest company costs you no more than the same policy in a weak one.

There is a form of baggage insurance, which may be taken by any one who travels. It is very inexpensive, and gives absolute protection, covering your baggage and personal effects in any part of the United States and Canada, on any railroad, train, baggage car, freight car, steamer or other vessel, coach, carriage, and in any storehouse, house, hotel, and club, or in any other likely place.

Do not over-insure or under-insure, but always insure for full value. If you over-insure you cannot get more than the value of the property burned, and you pay the extra cost for nothing.

Always carry a schedule of your property, even to the number of books insured, and place this paper in your safe, or, better, in a safe deposit box, or in some secure place away from the property insured. Do not leave your policies in a bureau drawer.

An insurance policy is supposed to cover the market value of the property at the time of its destruction, not necessarily what it will sell for, but what it can be replaced for; for example, you have a sideboard which cost you one hundred dollars. As a second-hand piece of furniture it would not sell for more than fifty dollars, but you can insure it for one hundred dollars or close to that sum. Articles which have a problematic value, like paintings and rare books, should be insured as works of art, and so specified in the policy.

CHAPTER XXVI

ACCIDENT INSURANCE

DURING the last quarter of a century, accident insurance has become somewhat universal and often epidemic. In some places this is due, not only to the fact that it has intrinsic value, but to the enterprise of the insurance companies.

Many people thoroughly believe in the necessity of carrying accident insurance, while others are opposed to it.

The fact that it is very inexpensive is indicative that accidents are rare. If they were frequent, the cost of the insurance would be much larger.

If you travel, or your work is hazardous, you should, most emphatically, take out an accident policy; but if you are not subject to more than ordinary risk it may not be worth while, although I can see no objection whatever to carrying it, particularly as the expense is small, and I think that I would favor it upon general principles.

If you are a working man or clerk dependent wholly upon your wages or salary, with no money, or little money, saved up, an accident policy may be considered a necessity. Many a poor man has been able to take care of his family, while sick from accident, because of his insurance.

It is well to read your policy over carefully. You may find that it is written in the interest of the company far more than in yours, and that it does not give all the protection that you think it does. Understand your policy before taking it. Show it to your lawyer or to some good business man. Understand what you are getting before you go to the expense of getting it.

CHAPTER XXVII

THE ANNUITY

THE annuity is a presumably safe but not common form of investment. It is similar to life insurance in general principles, but differs from it in that the holder of a straight life policy must usually die to win, while the man with an annuity must live to win.

An annuity is an agreement, made by an insurance or other guaranteeing company, to pay the annuity-holder a specified sum of money, by the month or by the year, so long as the holder of it may live.

Practically all life insurance policies are obtainable by the making of a first payment and continuous, periodical payments, but the annuity must be paid for wholly in advance.

The expense of life insurance is based upon age, the younger the insured, the smaller the cost. These conditions are reversed with annuities. The older the person, the less he pays for an annuity.

No physical examination is necessary, for, as a matter of fact, the older and weaker the person insured, the better it is for the insuring company.

Comparatively few annuities are taken out by other than aged people, those who are too old, as a rule, to continue in active business, and who prefer the guarantee of a stated sum for the balance of their lives to any other form of investment. Then, to many of these people, the annuity offers a larger income than it may be possible to obtain from the interest on the sum paid for the annuity; for example, it is possible to purchase an annuity large enough to live upon for, perhaps, twenty thousand dollars. Twenty thousand dollars, at five per cent, will yield an annual income of only one thousand dollars, which may not be sufficient for the comfortable support of the man who is considering an annuity.

By taking out an annuity in a first-class company, a comfortable income is assured for life, and the holder of it need give no thought to his financial future. But before buying an annuity it would be well for him to consider what his twenty thousand dollars is worth to him if he retains it. Perhaps it would be wiser for him to use the interest, and a part of the principal, than to take out an annuity, particularly if his days are numbered, and, provided, of course, that his money is well invested. The chances are that he will not outlive his money, and would, then, be able to leave something to relatives, friends, or charity, instead of paying it to the annuity company.

Each case must be considered by itself. Each must be weighed for both advantages and disadvantages.

I would suggest that if you are considering an annuity, you discuss the matter with your doctor and some good business friend, who are familiar with your circumstances. Together, you would probably arrive at a profitable conclusion.

CHAPTER XXVIII

BACKING BUSINESS

ACCURATE statistics are impossible, but it would appear to be self-evident that a proportion of those who start in business for themselves borrow a part of their working capital, obtaining it from banks, trust companies, friends, or from others.

It is of this "others" that I am writing,— those who would loan their money to men starting in business or who would enlarge their businesses.

This book is devoted to men of limited means, who are unable to save more than small sums. I do not propose to offer any suggestion to the large investor,— to the captain of industry, or to those who deal in money-lending. The professional money-lender makes a business of loaning money. Money to him is a commodity. He has it for sale. He is prepared to meet large or small losses, his profit depending upon the average safety of his investments, not upon the success of any one of them. He is under the protection of the law of averages.

Loss and risk are parts of the scheme of business-doing; but only the minimum risk should be taken by one of small income. If large risks are justifiable, they should be confined to those who can afford to lose, who know how to play the game of speculation, and who will not touch bottom if they meet with ordinary or occasional losses.

Altogether too often men of considerable means, and small investors, loan money to friends and acquaintances, who are about to start in business, or who desire to extend their business and have not the necessary capital for doing so. Sometimes this is done for friendship's sake, but more often on account of the high rate of interest paid, or the promise of large returns.

I consider this form of money-lending removed from investment, so far as the man of little money is concerned. At best, it is hazardous —

First, because the loaner is not likely to be capable of accurately diagnosing business conditions; he is not in a position to know the ins and outs of the business for which the money is to be loaned.

Secondly, he may be influenced either by friendship or by visionary expectation, and be led to believe that he will receive an exorbitant return for his loan.

Thirdly, it is unusually difficult to obtain good

security, or much of any except unreliable prospective.

Fourthly, the lack of judgment on the part of the borrower, or many other causes, may operate for loss.

Fifthly, his money is at arm's length; yes, more so; for it is altogether out of his reach. It is not like money in the bank, subject to draft; it is money where it cannot be called in when wanted.

Let me again impress upon the salary-receiver, wage-earner, and the man of low income, that they have no business or moral right to consider any form of investment which does not present the maximum, or close to the maximum, of security.

Unless one is financially able to take speculative chances, he should not place his money out of his control, except in the best of investment securities, or in making deposits where there is actual safety, or what is so considered by the best judges of investments.

True, when one deposits in the savings bank, or buys a government bond, his money passes into the control of others, and he is given no right to dictate the action of those who handle his savings. But his money is better protected than it would be if he had it, because it is in the hands of conservative and experienced men,—not any one man,—and subject to the care of a composite organization.

It should be borne in mind that about ninety per cent of the men in business for themselves either have failed or will fail during their career. True, many of them recover from disaster and become successful ultimately. But when accurate statistics show conclusively that bankruptcy, or some other form of failure, is sure to be the experience of nine-tenths of the men in business, it would appear obvious that the small money-saver had better not take so great a chance with his hard-earned accumulation.

A man may be justified in taking a little more than reasonable risk with his active money, — that money which he, himself, controls,—but it is certainly bad judgment to invest one's savings where they are unprotected, either by personal or composite security.

The man of small income should never back anybody's business, save his own, or loan money to anybody without ample security, unless the loan be out of friendship, and then only when the pressure of friendship, or the friend's necessities, are great enough to warrant the risk which sometimes friendship rightly requires.

Backing Business

Never loan money to anybody, under any circumstances, without security, unless you do it for love, and do not do it for love without taking yourself into consideration.

CHAPTER XXIX

KEEPING A BANK ACCOUNT

THERE are three kinds of banks of deposit: First, the national bank which cannot be capitalized for less than twenty-five thousand dollars, and is under the direct supervision of the United States Government. This supervision, however rigid it may be, does not, and cannot, guarantee the reliability of the bank, or secure the depositor against loss. It can, at best, but safeguard him, and operate as a protection. National banks fail, but, as a rule, fewer of them collapse than any other class of financial institutions. The depositor is a preferred creditor, and he must be paid first; therefore, when the bank fails, he is quite likely to receive all, or nearly all, of the money held on deposit, although he may be obliged to wait some time for all of it. Unless the collapse is almost complete, the other banks are likely to stand by the one in trouble, and to advance a large part of the deposited money, in which case the depositor would not have to wait more than a few days or weeks, except for a small percentage of what he had on deposit.

Secondly, trust companies, or loan and trust companies, which are institutions incorporated under State law, and subject only to State inspection. The larger and better trust companies are usually co-members with national banks of the local clearing houses, and are then subject to some supervision by the clearing-house officials. This supervision is quite likely to be very rigid, partly because the failure of a loan or trust company affiliated with the national banks is a direct injury to all members of the clearing house. As the laws in some States are not as strenuous as is the national bank law, it is quite probable that many loan and trust companies do not receive as thorough a supervision as is given to the national banks. But many large trust companies are officered by men of ability, integrity, and responsibility, and are as financially sound and as safe as are the majority of national banks.

Thirdly, the so-called State bank. This institution is practically the same as is the national bank, except that it is not under the supervision and inspection of the United States Government. As a matter of fact, there is very little difference between it and the loan and trust company.

National and State banks, and loan and trust companies, differ from savings banks in that they do a purely commercial business, the depositor or customer placing his money in the bank that he may draw it out by check at any time. The depositor is, besides, entitled to what is known as "accommodation," the bank agreeing to discount his paper and to loan him money from time to time, provided, of course, that the security offered by him, or his credit, justifies the loan.

The national bank issues bank bills or paper money. No other institution does it, although the State bank can legally do so, but is prevented by a prohibitory tax.

National banks do not, as a rule, pay interest on deposits subject to check, unless the account is somewhat inactive, or is very large.

An inactive account is one where the depositor does not make more than an occasional deposit, and draws comparatively few checks, and does not often borrow money from the bank. Because his account requires very little clerical work, some national banks pay interest on deposits if they average a thousand dollars. Practically, all State banks, trust companies, and loan and trust companies, pay their depositors two per cent on daily balances of not less than five hundred dollars, a few companies allowing interest on three hundred dollars, and some do not pay more than one and a half per cent. Occasionally, a trust company or State bank pays two and a half to three per cent on daily balances subject to check, but I do not believe that any well-managed institution can afford to give so high an interest rate. If it is paid, I am inclined to think that the bank is doing it at a loss, and any voluntary loss, unless the money involved is used for legitimate advertising or development purposes, does not speak well for the bank's standing and reliability.

Some State banks and loan and trust companies maintain a savings bank department, which is separate and distinct from the regular banking department.

The depositor places his money in a bank for two reasons:

First, that it may be secure.

Secondly, that he may use it as he wants it, drawing it out by check. This is a great convenience, as it obviates the necessity of carrying large sums of money on one's person, or of keeping it in the office or home, and is the best protection against robbery or other loss. It offers also the convenience of paying bills by check, and sending remittances by mail with the liability of loss reduced to a minimum. It has another advantage, which is of considerable consequence, for the depositor, if he carries a deposit of fair size, will be accommodated by the bank whenever he is short of money, provided, of course, that he can give security. No reputable bank ever takes more than the current rate of interest, and that is always far below that asked by loan agencies. The borrower usually makes out a note for the amount desired, carries it to the bank, and the officers or directors pass upon it. The note must either be endorsed by some reliable person, or else accompanied by some security,— stock, bonds, or the like. If the note is accepted, the face value of it is paid to the depositor, less the discount or interest. For example, let us suppose that you borrow a thousand dollars from your bank for four months at six per cent interest or discount. Six per cent interest per annum is two per cent for four months. The bank, therefore, instead of giving you one thousand dollars, gives you but nine hundred and eighty dollars, taking out of the thousand dollars in advance the interest or so-called discount. The note must be paid at maturity or renewed.

I would advise any one, if he has a sum of not less than two hundred dollars, to open an account in some good bank, and to pay all of his bills, excepting small ones, by check. Not only is this a great convenience, but it is more businesslike; it is a protection against loss; it offers a legal receipt for money paid out, provided the check is made payable to order and not to bearer, for the receiver cannot obtain his money unless he endorses the check, and this endorsement is a receipt.

A good banking connection is of great value to any one, whether he does business or not, whether he is a clerk or is in business for himself, or whether or not he needs a bank for borrowing purposes. A man with a bank account stands better in the community, in business and out of it. The mere fact that he has available bank money is *prima facie* evidence that he has some local standing. Even men with small incomes can save enough money, if they will, to start a checking account.

It is quite easy to ascertain the weakness or soundness of a bank. The character of the men in command counts for much. They are usually of high standing, rigid integrity, and progressive conservatism. Their position is known to other bankers, and bank officials are usually willing to give expert opinion of the standing of other institutions. The bank that is unknown is unsound, and its officers are ordinary business men, either of no standing at all or of little reputation.

Never deposit any money in the bank, large or small, until you have inquired about it. If it is all right, the majority of the business men in the town know about it. If it is shaky, responsible parties will refuse to recommend it.

As a rule, do not ask a professional man to

give his opinion of the character of a bank or other institution. Go to some well-known business man of character and standing. Better see two or more of these men. Naturally they know much about the inside of every bank in town, or they are acquainted with men who do know.

If there is no bank in your place of residence, and the nearest one is some miles away, you can easily obtain the rock-bottom facts. A letter addressed to any large national bank in a city will bring a courteous reply. Responsible bankers never speak well of weak institutions; they cannot afford to do so. Better write to two or three city banks. The names of the officers and directors of all reliable banking institutions are public property, and their reliability is known to every near-by banker and large business man.

There are scattered throughout the country, usually in small towns, banks of deposit owned and controlled by unreliable men with questionable reputations. Many of these banks are links of a chain of banks. Frequently they are controlled by one man, who is able, at any time, to wreck them. Unless you are a financial expert, your own opinion is worth very little. If a responsible business man or banker recommends the bank, your money may be placed there at the minimum of risk.

CHAPTER XXX

THE COÖPERATIVE BANK

THE coöperative bank is, as its name implies, a combination of men banded together for mutual interests and protection. It deals exclusively in real estate and real estate mortgages, its loans, as a rule, being confined to its members. Its capital is obtained by selling shares, each share-holder having full voting rights, and something to do with the management of the business and the investments.

The share-holders elect the proper officers and committees, whose province is to invest or loan the money, presumably at the very maximum of safety. They are not supposed to take any risk. There is usually little or no opportunity for embezzlement or irregularity, because little ready cash is on hand at any time, the money being let out immediately with its coming in.

All money is loaned, either by vote of the share-holders in meeting assembled, or by a large committee chosen by the share-holders.

Checks are not valid unless they bear several signatures.

The utmost caution is encouraged, and every

action is passed upon, leaving little opportunity for carelessness.

A share in a well-organized coöperative bank offers very good security, whether or not the owner intends to borrow money of the bank for building purposes. The principal danger, and perhaps the only danger, lies in the possible lack of judgment on the part of the officers and committees who invest the money. Should loans be made above the value of the property, a loss is likely to occur, and a continuous lack of judgment is pretty sure to wreck the bank.

Then, carelessness on the part of the local adviser or title-searcher may result in disaster. It is sometimes difficult to ascertain whether or not a title is good. An incompetent attorney may pass a weak title and pronounce it sound. But as its investigating and investing committees are large, and as all of the members are, or should be, familiar with the territory in which they live, and, further, as the bank is not likely to loan outside of its town or suburbs, there is ample opportunity for properly weighing values, and, consequently, less chance for the exercising of bad judgment.

The strength of the bank is dependent upon

the character of its members and the conservatism and judgment of its committees.

I would not advise any one to have anything to do with a coöperative bank which is officered or managed by speculators and financial manipulators, or with any bank which is apparently under the control of one man or of any one set of men.

If the bank is solid and well managed, its sound condition is known to the regular bankers and leading business men of the town. Unless these men will recommend the bank, keep away from it.

It is obvious, of course, that no well-managed coöperative bank can pay more than current rates of interest. The bank making, apparently, more than a fair rate of interest is probably unsound. The borrower, with good security, is never obliged to pay exceeding six per cent interest. If he pays more than that, he does it because the security he offers is not up to normal.

The coöperative bank is especially recommended to those about to build, who would then have an opportunity of borrowing from a combination of which they are a part.

If you are a member of a coöperative bank, attend all of its meetings, that you may keep track of what is being done.

CHAPTER XXXI

THE HOME BANK

THE old-time children's custom of keeping, and of sometimes filling, a little tin or iron bank, with pennies or other coins, has, during the last few years, broadened itself out to include the older people.

Hundreds and thousands of fathers and mothers, and young men and women, married and single, make it a point to deposit in one of these little home savings banks from a cent a day to a larger sum a week. Many make it their duty to drop into the bank all of the pennies they receive, or all of the five-cent pieces, or all of the ten-cent pieces.

This custom is to be encouraged, even among the well-to-do, for it allows one, almost unconsciously, to accumulate small or greater sums of money, which may be used for a specific purpose, or placed in the savings bank, or otherwise put away, whenever the amount is large enough for deposit or investment.

I would most emphatically advise the man of family, the wage-earner, and salary-receiver, to place on the dining-room shelf a tin or iron bank, and to make systematic visits to it; and, further, to have one for each of the children, and one for each of the grown-ups as well. Nothing contributes more to the principle of systematic saving. Its whole influence is good. It is one of the foundation stones of success.

But be systematic about it.

Better deposit one cent a day every day, than five cents occasionally.

Better put away every five-cent piece, and do it religiously, than to save only when the spirit moves.

Establish a basis, whether it be one cent a day or a dollar a day, and when you have established it, stick to it, unless the unforeseen occurs.

CHAPTER XXXII

KEEPING ACCOUNTS

EVERYBODY, in business or out of it, on the farm or in the store or office, in school as teacher or pupil, married or single, old or young,— if old enough to know the difference between subtraction and addition,— should keep some sort of a record of the money coming in and where it came from, and of the money going out and where it goes.

There is every reason for this, and absolutely not even the slightest shadow of an excuse for not doing it.

It is very necessary to know where money comes from and where it goes, whether one handles a few dollars a week, or a few million dollars a year. I am not asking the reader to take a course in bookkeeping, or even consider the art of double-entry. But what is known as "single entry" is as simple as the multiplication table, for all one has to do is to enter what he receives, and what he pays out, and strike a balance, which cannot help showing him whether he is running ahead or running behind, and enables him to locate with exactness necessary expense and unnecessary extravagance.

In no other way can he be familiar with his own financial condition, or ascertain whether or not he is spending too much or too little in any direction.

The mere keeping of accounts will not prevent extravagances, or careless expenditure, but it will locate the leaks, and this, by itself, works for economy.

No elaborate books are necessary. One book will do. In the first part of it, enter all the money you receive. Simply write:

1912	
Jan. 1, Salary	$22.00
Feb. 2, Interest from Blankville Savings Bank	19.40

Beginning in the middle of the book enter each item of expense, as:

1912	
Jan. 1, Rent	$26.00
Jan. 15, Groceries (Cobb & Cobb) . . .	3.68
Jan. 31, Lunches for the month	6.25

It is not necessary to enter every small expenditure by itself. For instance, if it costs you ten cents a day for carfare, make one entry for the month. And little things, like postage stamps and spent nickels, can be lumped together under "incidentals." But do not take too many liberties with incidentals. It is better to specify than to make blank entries, unless they are of very little significance.

At the end of each month strike a balance, and at the end of each year make up a little table of averages, of loss or gain. In this table you will include what you have saved.

If you are not a professional bookkeeper, and have never studied bookkeeping, I suggest that you ask some bookkeeper to give you a little assistance, to map out a sort of form for you to follow, so easy and so simple that you can readily fill it out. Do not let this bookkeeping friend work out for you any complicated scheme of keeping accounts. The simpler it is the better for you, provided it covers the ground.

Accurate statistics are impossible, but I think that I may claim that one half of the men, and ninety per cent of the women, either keep no record of expenses, or keep one which is a little worse than none at all. These foolish people will, if questioned, present one or more of the convenient, standard, kiln-dried, and mildewed excuses. Most of them will say that they have not the time. Ninety-nine per cent of those who use this excuse refuse to keep proper accounts from pure, unadulterated laziness, unwillingness to handle time as a commodity, and a lack of appreciation of established principles of economy.

The only class of people who have plenty of time for everything are those who are extremely busy. If you want anything done, ask a busy man to do it for you, not the loafer.

Another excuse, which is not quite so dry as the foregoing, is that one can tell what he has by counting what he has left over; that is to say, if his income is fifty dollars a month and he has eight dollars left over at the end of the month, his expenses have been forty-two dollars. This excuse is unworthy of any consideration, and laziness is back of it. It is important to know how much we have left over, but not more so than it is to know how it happens that we do not have more or less left over.

Another prevalent and thoroughly idiotic excuse is used by the careless and lazy, who claim that knowing where money comes from and where it goes does no good, either in expenditure or in saving. The absurdity of this claim is too great for even passing comment.

While there are hundreds of thousands of men and women who do not understand bookkeeping, and who do not keep complete or even fair accounts, it is a fact that practically all systematic and successful savers, those who respect and recognize the responsibilities of the present and future, those who are wise enough and honest enough to protect themselves for the good of themselves and the community, keep some sort of account of income and outgo, and regulate their financial affairs with some degree of system.

I do not mean to say that every spendthrift, and that all improvident and irresponsible people, do not keep a record of their financial affairs, but I never knew a spendthrift, or any other careless handler of money, who took any account of what came in and what went out.

The keeping of accounts is absolutely necessary to the proper and economical management of financial affairs, and to systematic saving and accumulation.

CHAPTER XXXIII

TREATING

I HAVE not considered treating under the chapter headed "Petty Extravagances." It has become so common, and has been responsible for so great a waste of money, that it should be discussed by itself. I am inclined to feel that treating has become epidemic, and that its practice is increasing.

There is a difference between the showing of necessary courtesy and the practice of indiscriminate courtesy, which is commonly called treating.

Treating does not create or maintain friendship. Its effect, in the end, is likely to be diametrically opposed to friendship. When it goes beyond the courtesy line, it is clear and sheer foolishness, is without excuse, is saturated with extravagance, and is often criminally wrong.

Hundreds and thousands of men could save considerable money if they gave up treating, not only their friends, but their acquaintances.

In the first place, treating is an inexcusable and expensive habit. The treater almost invariably spends his money for things he does not need, and he is obliged to partake of those things at his own expense every time that he treats another.

Comparatively few men like to drink alone, and very few become intoxicated from the solitary bottle. Ninety per cent of intoxication and liquor drinking is done at the open bar, at the dining-table, or where men congregate; and the man who would take but one drink, takes a dozen, because of the habit of treating. It is so with smoking, and with other habits, but it is largely confined to drinking.

I do not propose to deliver a temperance lecture. It would be out of place in a book like this. But I am considering liquor drinking and treating as prevalent and inexcusable extravagances.

The habitual drinker or treater does not, and cannot, as a rule, provide for his future.

Liquor drinking is the fore-runner of degradation, and is an unrelenting enemy of every form of economy, and a most successful agent of extravagance.

Alcohol has its place, but there is, from every standpoint, moral and material, no excuse for the habitual drinking of liquor as a beverage, and the drinker, and especially the treating drinker, cannot forge ahead, and he is not likely to be able to provide for the future.

It is a fact that the higher grade of men are

the least addicted to treating. They may do it occasionally as a courtesy, and some of them may be moderate drinkers; but the rank and file of them pay their bills, earn the money which they spend, and spend it carefully, always with the exercise of good judgment.

No one but the habitual treater has any respect for the habitual treater, and I do not think that even he has much of any for his kind.

Friendship that comes from promiscuous treating, from any kind of mental or physical debauchery, is the weakest sort of friendship, and is without staple foundation.

CHAPTER XXXIV

THE SAFE DEPOSIT BOX

I WOULD advise every one, excepting those who have practically no property, to rent a safe deposit box.

Safe deposit companies are located in every large city, and many country banks maintain safe deposit departments.

So far as I know, nothing placed in a safe deposit box has ever been lost except through the carelessness of its owner.

It is practically impossible to burglarize the vault containing safe deposit boxes: First, because they are made with the greatest care. Secondly, because they are usually protected by day and night watchmen, electric burglar alarms, and lights. Thirdly, because only the highest grade of professional burglar can possibly get into them, and he is not likely to know the contents of any one box. He must break into the strongest vaults, and pass the attendants, safety alarms, and outside interference, and he must then open each box separately; and, after all, he is just as likely to force a vacant box as one containing securities.

It would seem that there might be some danger, — that the attendant, knowing the renters, might get into the box; but, so far as I know, this has never occurred. In the first place, two keys are required, the attendant's key and the renter's key. The attendants are selected with every precaution, and it would be very difficult for any one of them to commit burglary without conniving with his associates.

Boxes large enough to hold any reasonable amount of property can be rented for from three to ten dollars a year. If the wage-earner feels that he cannot afford the price of a box, and holds valuable papers, I would suggest that he wrap them up carefully, with his name and address in his own handwriting on the outside of the package, and ask a reliable banker to hold them for him. Of course, there is a little risk here, but not so great as there would be if the papers were left about the house.

CHAPTER XXXV

WHAT SOME TERMS STAND FOR

ABOVE Par.— Above par, or more than par value, usually applies to stocks and bonds which are quoted, sold, or valued at more than their face value. For example, if a stock, with a par or face value of a hundred dollars, is worth or is sold for more than a hundred dollars, such stock is said to be "Above Par."

Assessment.— Holders of stock, other than non-assessable stock, can usually be called upon to pay an additional sum, after they have purchased the stock, and this is called an assessment. It is well to avoid purchasing stock that is not non-assessable. The certificates of non-assessable stock contain the word "Non-Assessable."

Bear.— Those who operate for declining prices are called "Bears." "Bearing the market" means to attempt to force down the prices of stocks and other securities.

Block.— This term is applied to a number of shares of stocks or bonds of the same kind and bought at the same time.

Board.— A short designation for the stock exchange, or stock board, or place where stocks and bonds are sold, other than a banker's or broker's office.

Bond.— A certificate running for a definite and specified period, which acts as a legal receipt for money borrowed by any government or corporation, and upon which interest is payable at a specified rate at specified intervals. The bond may be secured by a mortgage or other lien upon the property. Bonds, as they run, offer better security than do stocks and usually pay a much lower rate of interest, which is fixed; while stocks, other than preferred, do not guarantee any specified rate, and may pay up to several hundred per cent. But it should be borne in mind that any guarantee written upon the certificate is worthless if it represents property of little or no value.

Break.— A quick and unexpected decline in the price of stocks or other securities.

Broker.— One who makes it his business to buy or sell any form of securities, his remuneration coming from commissions. He is distinct from a banker, although one may be both a broker and a banker. Brokers who deal in stocks and bonds are sometimes called " stock brokers " or " bond brokers."

Bull.— One who operates, or who attempts to operate, the stock market for advancing prices.

To " bull the market " means to attempt to force the prices above normal.

Call-Loans.— Money loaned subject to demand; that is to say, the lender may demand his money without giving advance notice, although most call-loans are not considered payable in less than from one to three days.

Capital.— The capital of a corporation is the fund which is used for the practice of its business, and includes all of its property, both real estate and all other assets. A company incorporated for, say, a hundred thousand dollars, is supposed to have property or funds to that amount, occasionally more; but the majority of corporations, making much effort to sell their stocks, have very much less in real assets than the amount of their capital, many companies being capitalized for a thousand times the value of what they are supposed to own. Under the loose laws of some of our States a corporation may be formed with an " expressed " capital of a hundred millions of dollars, and yet its assets and the actual extent of its property may be limited to a hole in the ground and a patented but useless pick.

Capital Stock.— The sum fixed by the charter of a corporation as the amount paid in by the stockholders. In some States it must be paid in cash, but in others it may be paid in worthless options or patents.

Certified Check.— A check which has been presented to the bank, but not cashed. Some officer of the bank, usually the cashier, stamps across it the word, "Certified," and below it writes his official signature. So far as the receiver of the check is concerned, this check is no longer a personal one, but is in reality a certificate of deposit, the failure of the one drawing it in no way vitiating it; but the depositor, or one drawing the check, is liable should the bank fail, if he personally presents the certified check in payment, while he is exempt from liability if the receiver of it has asked the bank to certify it.

Chattel Mortgage.— A mortgage on personal property, such as furniture, horses, carriages, stock in trade, and almost everything else except real estate.

Commercial Paper.— A term applied to notes given in business which are negotiable, that is, can be sold.

Common Stock.— Stock which entitles one to equal dividends of the profits, if there be any, after the payment of dividends to the preferred stockholders.

Corner.— The expression "cornering the market" applies to the condition of the stock market, when certain stocks are purchased in sufficient quantities to allow the buyers of them to control the price.

Coupons.— Detachable slips, which are a part of some bonds, on which one receives the interest due at specified times. They are to be cut off, and presented for payment on the dates printed upon them.

Curb Market.— A place of trading in stocks and bonds, usually located upon the street (hence its name), in which are bought and sold stocks or other securities which are not recognized by the regular stock exchange or stock board. So-called "curb stocks" are likely to be of questionable value, and are, at best, considered highly speculative. The small investor had better keep away from all stocks or other securities sold on the "curb."

Debenture Bonds.— Bonds that have no material or tangible security back of them save that of good-will, good intentions, and reputation.

Dividend.— That part of the profits which is divided among the stockholders.

Fully-paid Stock.— The stock which has been paid for in cash or in property, or in some recognized or legal equivalent, and is not, therefore, assessable.

Future.— The buyer's right to demand delivery, and the seller's right to deliver, within a certain specified time.

Lamb.— A term applied to inexperienced stock buyers and speculators. The word "fool" would be more appropriate.

Listed Stocks and Bonds.— Securities that are recommended and sold by the regular stock exchanges and stock boards, and are not subject to the usual fluctuations of purely speculative stocks; but it must not be understood that the value of "listed stocks" is guaranteed. Thousands of men have been ruined by buying only what were supposed to be reliable stocks and bonds.

Long.— One is called "long on the market" when he has bought stock with the expectation of an advance in price.

Margin.— Stock is said to be purchased "on margin" when the customer pays down only a part of the price, the usual payment being ten per cent, which is supposed to cover any probable decline within the next few days. Ninety out of every hundred failures are due to buying stock "on margin."

Mortgage.— A mortgage is practically a bill-of-sale, but the mortgagee cannot obtain the property until the expiration of the mortgage, provided the interest is paid regularly, nor can he obtain it without a foreclosure, and the mortgagor has a right to redeem his property at the expiration, if he pays the principal and interest.

Mortgagee.— One who lends money on a mortgage, who takes a mortgage as security.

Mortgagor.— One who mortgages his property.

Par.— The face or written value of anything, but usually applied to stocks and bonds. First-class stocks generally have a par value of one hundred dollars.

Point.— Applies to one dollar a share. When stock advances ten points, for example, it is said to be worth ten dollars more than its former price.

Pool.— Large quantities of any stock bought together for putting through some deal.

Preferred Stock.— Stock which entitles the owner to dividends out of the net profits before anything is paid to the regular stockholders, that is, the holders of what is known as "common stock." Preferred stockholders have also the advantage over the others should the company be dissolved. Preferred stock can never pay a dividend above that specified upon the face of the certificate, no matter how large the profits of the company may be.

Private Corporations.— Business concerns doing business with private capital and under private management, and not amenable to legislative control beyond the laws covering general corporations. These companies include practically all business houses or combinations other than partnerships.

Public Corporations.— Municipal or State organizations.

Quasi-Public Corporations.— Those which operate under franchise, such as telephone, telegraph, railroad, gas, and water companies. Although they are private corporations they are somewhat under government control.

Selling Short.— When one sells at a price with the expectation of buying a stock at a lower price and making delivery, he is said to be "selling short."

Share.— A stock certificate, or any other certificate, representing a part of the capital stock.

Sinking Fund.— A definite sum of money set aside for a specific purpose.

Syndicate.— A combination of men formed for the purpose of putting through some business deal.

Underwriting.— A banker, or group of bankers and manipulators, who purchase an entire bond issue at a specific price, with the expectation of retailing the bonds at a higher price.

Watered Stock.— When stock is issued in excess of the tangible property, the security is said to be " watered."

Working Capital.— That portion of the capital of the corporation, or other concern, used directly for the doing of its business.

Treasury Stock.— That part of the capital stock which has not been sold, but has been held in the treasury of the company to be disposed of from time to time as the necessities of the business warrant, the proceeds of the sale to go into the business.

THE END

INDEX

Index

Spotted something that isn't quite right?

Let us know and we'll fix it for future reprints.
And as a thank you for your diligence, we'll
send you a free Sothis book of your choice.

publisher@sothis.press

This page intentionally left blank

Made in the USA
Monee, IL
08 November 2026

68113585R00173